Perched Like Doves

Greta Barnes continued her nursing career while she was bringing up her three children, working part time as a staff nurse and district nurse. When the children were established at school she became the nurse co-ordinator of the Medical Research Council's Hypertension Trial and subsequently a specialist nurse, lecturer and researcher in the management of asthma, diabetes and hypertension in the community.

From 1986 until her retirement in 2001 she was the Founder/Director of the National Asthma and Respiratory Training Centre [now known as Education for Health] which was based firstly in Stratford-upon-Avon and then moved to larger premises in Warwick in 1997.

She was appointed MBE in 1995 and received the European Respiratory Society Presidential Award in 2006 and the British Thoracic Society Medal in 2016.

Her daily diary of hospital life which she kept whilst she was a student nurse from 1959-1962, resulted in the publication of *Scissors, Nurse, Scissors* and subsequently she compiled and edited *The Heart of Barts*, a pot-pourri of memories from the 1930s to the 1970s. Her book *Long Live Barts*, about the early years at the hospital from 1123-1900 was published in 2013.

Greta Barnes and her husband David live in a small Cotswold village and have a large close family including nine grandchildren for whom, when they were younger, she wrote the book *What can I do now Granny?*

PERCHED LIKE DOVES

Greta Barnes

Matador
9 Priory Business Park,
Wistow Road, Kibworth Beauchamp,
Leicestershire. LE8 0RX
Tel: 0116 279 2299
Email: books@troubador.co.uk
Web: www.troubador.co.uk/matador
Twitter: @matadorbooks

ISBN 978 1789015 515

British Library Cataloguing in Publication Data.
A catalogue record for this book is available from the British Library.

Printed and bound by CPI Group (UK) Ltd, Croydon, CR0 4YY
Typeset in 11 Minion Pro by Troubador Publishing Ltd, Leicester, UK

Matador is an imprint of Troubador Publishing Ltd

For David

'Technical skill alone will make a nurse but when combined with sympathy, and the charm of gracious manners, it makes the great nurse'.

Isla Stewart, *British Journal of Nurses*, 4th June 1904

Contents

Prologue

It was too late to reach the safety of the air raid shelter. The bombs rained down relentlessly. My mother went into instant, powerful labour, and I made my entrance into the world at 3.40am on the morning of 15th December 1940 in the middle of a ferocious air raid. Kicking, screaming and scrawny, I was, by all accounts, not a pretty sight.

The maternity nurse cheerily reassured my mother, 'There is an old adage which says, "Ugly in the cradle, lovely at the table".'

I was given my name immediately in case of need. It had already been decided that if I were a girl I would be called Greta, named reputedly after a beautiful blonde whom my father had met when he was on business in Sweden. My mother was quite happy with this, but my paternal grandmother was furious and never ever called me Greta, but always by my second name, Rosemary.

The all-clear siren sounded. My mother wept; whether this was due to my ugliness, exhaustion from giving birth, or from sheer relief that we had survived the bombing that night unscathed, I will never know.

*

The war was still raging in 1944, and on my fourth birthday I was suffering from a bad attack of measles. I was lying in bed, spotty and miserable, and the blackout curtains had been drawn to protect my eyes. For my birthday present, my parents had been delighted to find a second-hand teddy bear. There was no gift wrapping paper during the war, so they wrapped the bear in already used, but ironed, brown paper and tied it up with household string. They presented it to me on my sick bed and watched in anticipation as I tore off the wrapping. I was confronted by a large, mangy, bedraggled, old bear with one eye and a damaged nose and arm.

'I don't want that.'

I sobbed and put my head under the bedclothes and went back to sleep. When I awoke some hours later, I found the bear tucked in beside me, and even at the tender age of four, I felt a great sense of guilt for being so unkind to this sorry creature. I immediately named him Bertie and promised him my undying love and devotion.

Throughout my childhood, I "nursed" Bertie, along with many of my dolls, in a specially created ward in our boxroom. Assorted cardboard boxes, with their lids removed, were lined up in neat rows on my hospital ward, and the necessary and numerous nursing tasks were carried out on a daily basis. My smart uniform consisted of an apron made from a torn linen sheet, on which had been painted a rather crooked red cross, and a cap made from a square damask table napkin, folded into a triangle and pinned at the back. My "Sister's" desk was a rickety dressing table, carefully positioned so I could keep an eye on all the patients.

Now, over seventy years later, Bertie continues to be in "good health" as he reclines on his comfortable armchair. His fur still bears the scars of my energetic surgery and enthusiastic ministrations over the years, and I love him all the more for it, for it was this damaged old toy which was undoubtedly the inspiration that set me off on my life's path.

Chapter One

Carcasses and Cockneys

I was seventeen when I first fell in love with London's East End. It was Thursday, 28th March, 1958, and I was feeling quite grown up as I walked under the archway of Smithfield Meat Market. I was instantly bewildered by how a place that was teeming with life could reek so of death and destruction. I looked up, and as far as I could see there were hundreds and hundreds of carcasses hanging upside down, swaying from their hooks. I watched, fascinated, as cheery bummarees, in their caps and smocks, rushed around carrying dead animals on their broad shoulders to the waiting distribution lorries.

The sun glinted off the blade being sharpened by a nearby butcher.

'Care for a butcher's, darlin'?'

His friendly smile drew me in as he cut deep into the flesh of what looked like a pig, before dismembering the animal into joint-sized pieces. Working with speed and dexterity, and a touch of theatre thrown in for his customer's enjoyment, he completed the amputations with a flourish and wiped his hands on his bloodied apron. I wondered if all surgeons showed such pride as they wielded their scalpels.

I could linger no longer and I left the meat market to visit the nearby Victorian public conveniences. The attendant was a delightful cockney woman, who I guessed was in her late fifties. She was wearing green overalls and a turban-style floral headscarf knotted at the front. As I was drying my hands on the towel she had given me, she said, 'Good luck today.'

I looked at her in astonishment. 'Thank you, but why wish me luck?'

She put her finger to her nose and smiled a smile laden with experience. 'It's Thursday, me duck, and interviews at the hospital are always on Thursdays. I'll have a few more like you in here today, titivating themselves up, and I'd wager all of you are off to Barts.'

She was right. I was on my way to my interview at St Bartholomew's Hospital – Barts, one of the most famous teaching hospitals in the world.

She looked me up and down. 'You'll get in; you look and talk proper. I've been looking after these lavs since before you was born or even a glimmer in your da's eye, and I can tell you, I know the ones they'll pick and the ones they won't.'

I looked in the mirror, seeing myself through her eyes in my brand new, brown Harris Tweed suit which my mother and I had chosen with great care. My sensible flat maroon shoes, along with my handbag and gloves, completed the ensemble. On the journey down from rural Warwickshire, I had begun to worry that my outfit was too countrified for London, but by then it was too late.

The fortune teller-cum-lavatory attendant's comments, which I was sure were meant to be reassuring, did little to bolster my confidence, and my washed hands were already becoming clammy. Then I started to worry that the wetness would cause the dye from my gloves to run, leaving me with embarrassingly red hands. There was nothing for it but to go before I lost my nerve altogether.

I made my way to the main gate of the hospital with my stomach churning and with the inside of my mouth feeling cardboard-dry. Glancing up, I noticed King Henry VIII, in all his majesty, positioned above the entrance staring down at me. He was standing with his legs apart, regally surveying all before him, as well he might, for I knew it was he who had kept the hospital open for the sick and poor of the City of London during the Reformation 400 years ago. I wondered what he would have made of me, a young girl in the 1950s.

At first glance, the gate seemed impenetrable, but it was opened immediately by a smartly dressed porter wearing a uniform with Barts-crested buttons, a peaked cap and immaculate white gloves.

'Here for an interview, are you?' He ticked my name off a list and directed me to the Nurses' Home.

I walked under an arch and entered a breathtakingly beautiful Square. I was to learn later that this little paradise was known as the "finest outdoor room" in England. The Square

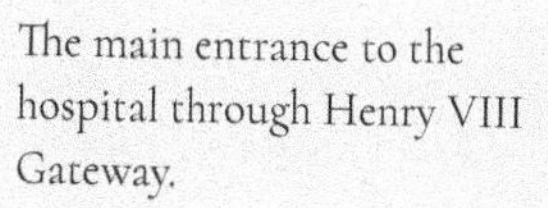

The main entrance to the hospital through Henry VIII Gateway.

housed some large, splendid plane trees, and at its centre stood a magnificent fountain adorned with fish heads as well as cherubs holding shells from which the sparkling water cascaded before resting peacefully in the circular pool below. Uniformed nurses wearing pretty fan-tailed white caps were sitting on the rim of the fountain, perched like resting doves as they chatted and laughed together.

As well as the nurses, there were *real* doctors on their way to save their patients' lives. They were easy to spot as their pristine white coats spread-eagled after them as they moved through the space with a clear air of superiority. Their splendour was unmatched by the male medical students, all of whom appeared creased and unwashed, with stethoscopes trailing nonchalantly from their pockets. These young men were in no hurry as they loitered around the fountain and tried to attract the attention of the fluttering "doves". Against this sea of white flashed the occasional pop of colour as patients, wrapped in red woollen blankets, were pushed through the Square in wheelchairs by the porters. I was momentarily mesmerised until I remembered my own reason for being there.

I made my way to the Nurses' Home and was ushered into a dingy and windowless room, where I joined a group of seven, similarly attired girls who were already seated on the hard wooden chairs lining the room's walls. Silence prevailed until a very pale individual suddenly said, 'I am really nervous and I think I'm going to be sick,' and, without delay, fled to find the nearest cloakroom, never to be seen again.

The interviews started, and having the surname Tisdale, I knew I would be one of the last. The Home Sister came in and out, escorting the next hopeful. In her long-sleeved royal blue uniform dress and stiff white cuffs, with her hair entirely swallowed up by her cap,

The Square known as the finest outdoor room in England.

Matron; the statuesque Miss Joan Loveridge.

she cut a very severe figure, and her manner did nothing to ease my discomfort. By the time nearly half the candidates had been called in, the heat and tension had begun to rise and the airless room became almost unbearable. I was the last to be called.

The Matron and Superintendent of Nursing, Miss Joan Loveridge, was a woman of large stature, which was magnified by her classic black uniform dress and a huge triangular white muslin cap. Although she was sitting at a desk, I could see through the knee hole that her swollen legs and feet were encased in sheer black nylon stockings. She had a kindly face and disposition, and I found myself relaxing a little for the first time that afternoon. She started the interview by telling me that St Bartholomew's Hospital only accepted one out of ten candidates who applied to the Nursing School and I began to wonder if she was already preparing me for failure.

'Now then, Miss Tisdale, tell me; why do you want to be a nurse?'

I had known this question was coming, but the words that stumbled out of my mouth were the hackneyed 'I've always wanted to help people.' I knew that this was not an answer to impress.

'Yes, and why else?' she probed.

'I have heard that young women choose to go to St Thomas's

Hospital for their training if they are a "lady", to Guy's Hospital if they want to have a good time, and to Barts if they want to be a good nurse – and I want to be a good nurse.'

My answer seemed to go down quite well. Thankfully, I didn't mention that having observed her nurses congregated around the fountain in their attractive uniforms and pretty tailed caps, I yearned to be a member of their coterie. I was too self-conscious, and it would have sounded so childish, to mention Bertie the bear: the real inspiration behind my nursing "vocation". Nor did I tell anyone else, until today, for that matter.

The interview was over. Matron gave no indication as to whether or not I had been successful, but I was informed that all the candidates would be sitting a test in maths and English during the course of the afternoon to check their academic ability. Meanwhile, I was invited to go to the Nurses' Dining Room for lunch, and I set off with the others, feeling fairly pessimistic about my chances.

*

Matron wrote to me on April Fool's Day 1958 to tell me my application for a vacancy as a Student Nurse at St Bartholomew's Hospital had been accepted, and arrangements had been made to receive me at the Preliminary Training School on 4th May 1959. She added that she hoped I would have a successful and happy training.

And so my future was assured, or so I thought.

*

I had time to fill until I was eighteen and a half (the minimum age of entry at the hospital) and I began to work very happily as a teacher's assistant in a local primary school for the next year. After a few very enjoyable months, it seemed as though things were going to plan; and then polio struck.

At the time, there was no vaccine available to prevent poliomyelitis, and epidemics of this horrific disease were rife, leading to many deaths in children and adults alike. Severe cases suffered from paralysis of the respiratory muscles, which meant they had to be nursed in an iron lung – a cylindrical steel drum that fitted over the patient's body. Prolonged artificial respiration was achieved by means of a mechanical pump, and, for many, survival depended on this apparatus for months or years and sometimes for a lifetime.

I was one of the lucky ones. Fortunately, I was only ill for six months and made a virtually full recovery. However, my doctor had to declare my illness on the medical certificate required by the hospital, and I was summoned to see a professor of neurology. My heart sank. Was my nursing career finished before it had even started? I didn't want to believe I had reached the final hurdle only to find it snatched away at the last minute. Various tests were performed and I had to stay overnight in the Nurses' Home to wait for the results. I slept badly, kept awake by trying to second-guess the outcome – the neurologist's examination had been thorough and I began to be convinced there was a problem. I felt slightly more optimistic, though, when I remembered a story about another girl who wanted to become a student nurse at the hospital. Her little fingers were both crooked and she was referred by the Matron to the orthopaedic surgeon to check her range of movement and the strength of the digits. The surgeon made the girl grip his finger with her little one. 'Good enough to pull corks out of bottles!' he declared and told Matron to accept her – and she did.

At last, I was summoned to Matron's office and the news was good. The eminent neurologist had noted a missing reflex in my left knee, but the rest of the tests were satisfactory, and this loss was not considered serious enough to stop me from embarking on a rigorous nurses' training course. Relief washed over me, until I remembered a conversation I had had the evening before.

*

I had been sitting in the large, graciously appointed Nurses' Sitting Room when I had met a second-year nurse called Downton. She had come to prepare the room for the Scottish Dancing Society and invited me to join the group. So, I ended up dancing the *Gay Gordons* to a record being played on an ancient gramophone, and at the end of the evening Nurse Downton had taken me to one side.

'Let me give you some advice,' she confided. 'Whatever you do, don't take up nursing; it's very hard work, your feet will kill you and I hate it.'

Her words echoed around my head. I had *always* wanted to be a nurse, and I was now being given a second chance at the hospital of my choice. I should have been carefree, but her comments had cast a shadow.

However, three months later I had forgotten all about Nurse Downton as I began to prepare for the most important day of my young life. My father's battered pale green trunk was brought down from the attic. His initials remained beautifully embossed across the lid. It had been well used, first by him when he was away at school and later by my brother. Now it was my turn. I don't know how many times I packed and unpacked; it could have been as many as ten times over a period of a few weeks. I had an ongoing compulsion to view my recently purchased prized possessions, particularly the two pairs of black seamed nylon stockings that had been bought from PH Woodward in

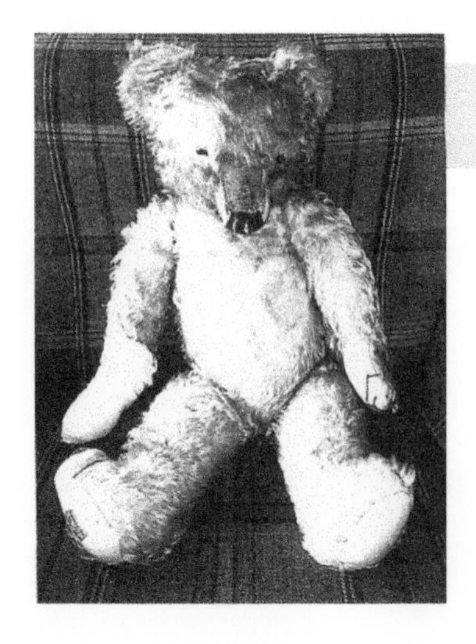

Bertie the Bear, all bandaged up and ready to go.

Leamington Spa. I couldn't resist the temptation to try them on. As I lifted them from the packet they were soft to the touch, and their rich blackness sent a tingle of anticipation across my skin. I couldn't decide whether they should be packed at the bottom of the trunk to show how relaxed I was about my future career, or on the top to show my vocational intent. These black stockings were, after all, the only evidence I had to show that I was off to "save the world". All the other items that needed to be included in my luggage were insignificant, apart from Bertie. He was worn with care, having been nursed back to life so many times over the years, and now I wrapped him up again and nestled him among my clothes to remind me that my childhood games were becoming a reality.

The trunk was sent by carrier to the Preliminary Training School at Letchmore Heath several days before I set out on my venture. It was too late to back out now.

Chapter Two

Pinned, Pleated, and Pinned Again

Monday morning, 4th May, 1959, and I was ready to go. The wait had seemed interminable, but at last I was on my way to the Preliminary Training School (PTS) of St Bartholomew's Hospital which was based in Hertfordshire. Rather bizarrely, it had been requested that I should carry an umbrella on my journey. I was therefore the proud possessor of a new, unwieldy, crook-handled scarlet item which seemed already to have a life of its own. Not wishing to fail my first instruction, I tucked the crook firmly over my wrist and set forth.

On arrival at Paddington Station, I took the underground to St Pancras where the concourse seemed to be full of people carrying umbrellas in spite of the bright summery weather. There were the usual upright, elegant men wearing bowler hats carrying their ubiquitous black umbrellas, but it was the flashes of colour amid the sombre sea of grey that caught my eye.

It seemed as if every solitary and lost young woman in London was clutching an umbrella at that moment, drawing strength from its solidity as the wave of passengers passed by. Once or twice, these fellow waifs shared tentative smiles as kindred souls sought each other out. The "identification" parade was complete when we all found ourselves on the same platform, catching the same train, at the same time.

The compartment accommodated eight. The seats were sagging and shabbily upholstered in a threadbare dark brown moquette. Four sepia photographs, all of seaside resorts that seemed a far-off promise, hung above the seats. Our collection of umbrellas, now safely stowed in the luggage rack, offered the only splash of colour in this brown box. And there I sat, with seven others, in total silence. The train's clickety-clack, clickety-clack, clickety-clack, sounded repeatedly in my head as, *You've made a mistake, you've made a mistake, you've made a mistake.* My heart sank as we rolled through the suburbs of London into the open green countryside. Smuts and soot streamed through the open window, and we continued to sit, wary and watchful, without speaking.

Waiting for us at Radlett Station in Hertfordshire was a row of taxis to transport us to our destiny – Piggotts Manor at Letchmore Heath. By now, the occupants of my compartment, who had been so quiet on the train, were all on first name terms and I was beginning to relax, but this was about to change.

An imperious figure was framed by a grand old oak door of the manor house, awaiting our arrival. She was wearing a long-sleeved royal blue uniform, with which I would soon become all too familiar, as well as the traditional flowing cap which floated past her thickening waist and covered all but the very front of her hair. She was none other than the Senior Sister Tutor whose name, I learnt later, was Miss Cape. She shook my hand regally.

'Good Afternoon, Nurse Tisdale.' *What* did she say? *Nurse* Tisdale? It was as much as I could do not to curtsey as she moved on to greet her next subject.

I was rather disappointed to find that the stately mock-Tudor building which housed the PTS was situated in the middle of the peaceful leafy Hertfordshire countryside and bore little resemblance, as far as I could see, to a busy teaching hospital in the East End of London and instead had the appearance of a rather grand country hotel. There were no patients in evidence and none of the hustle and bustle [or, indeed, the romance] that had thrilled me on my first visit to the Square at Barts. I began to worry that we wouldn't even get to wear the uniform that I spent so long dreaming about.

Nevertheless, Piggotts Manor had wonderful features – the glorious grounds included manicured lawns, well-tended rose beds and herbaceous borders, as well as a lake and two tennis courts. After a five-minute walk through the manor's vegetable gardens and its orchard bedecked with pink and white apple blossom, Aldenham Cottage came into view. It was here, where the space belied the name, we were to eat four delicious

Piggotts Manor, a splendid establishment situated in the heart of the country.

meals a day, all prepared by the in-house cook. Afternoon tea served in the dining room was to prove irresistible as the air filled with the tantalising aroma of warm, freshly home-baked bread, which we spread thickly with butter and sweet raspberry jam. The joy of tea at Aldenham Cottage was so much more than the food; it was through sharing in the slicing of the large loaves and enjoying this momentary relief from the tension of training that our future friendships were formed.

There were only two shops in Letchmore Heath and both catered for "everything the nurses wanted". Their stock ranged from the white Kirby grips, essential for keeping our caps in place and our hair behind our ears, to a small lending library. The novels all appeared to end happily with the doctor and nurse falling in love as their eyes met over their masks in the operating theatre. None of us joined the library – it would have been too embarrassing for words.

I was told I would be sleeping in Room 12 and would be sharing with a Nurse Grunsell, who I soon discovered was called Beth. On first acquaintance, Beth, who was very quietly spoken, appeared serious, studious and shy. Within minutes, though, I could see she had a distinctive sense of humour, and I felt confident she would be a good roommate. She wasted no time in telling me her chief dislike: 'I don't like getting up in the morning and I can't speak to *anyone* before I've had breakfast.' No early morning chats for us then; she was obviously the owl as I was the lark.

Room 12 was in the eaves, up two flights of stairs and obviously in what had been the servants' quarters during the manor's grander days. Our beds were squashed into the room with barely a breath's space between them and were complete with hard horsehair mattresses that offered little comfort. Nevertheless, my ability to sleep soundly was never in question. The room itself had little to recommend it with its brown linoleum floor and lack of washing facilities. Later, we found that the bedrooms on the lower floors were really quite luxurious and had carpets and wash basins, but all things considered, we felt no envy as we quickly began to feel at home in our little eyrie. Bertie Bear took pride of place on my bed and Beth, who was a keen campanologist, strung a red, white and blue bell rope – with its distinctive churchy scent – around the edge of our mirror.

To my relief, I found, contrary to my worries, we *were* going to wear uniforms. They were discovered stowed away in the chest of drawers, starched and neatly folded, daring us to commit our first sins and soil them. We were instructed to put them on, after which we would be shown how to make our caps. "Nurse" Grunsell and I took one look at the various items and fell into uncontrollable nervous laughter. A *real* uniform – this was getting serious. We had three dresses each, fourteen aprons, three belts, a navy cape lined romantically in red, numerous collars and cuffs (which would need sewing onto the dresses each time the dress was laundered) and caps. Except the caps weren't caps at all; they were just squares of fine starched material of brilliant white cotton. We struggled into our uniform dresses, which had to be fastened with a long row of stiff rubber buttons, but unfortunately we hadn't realised that first we should have attached the collar, so we had to begin again. Next came the apron, which required four safety pins; this in itself was a problem as Beth had mislaid her stock and I had temporarily lost the key to my trunk.

Then it was time for those precious black stockings, which were held up by a suspender belt. Each stocking was joined at the back with a seam that had to be worn precisely up the centre of the back of the leg – requiring a rather tricky manoeuvre. We had not yet acquired our regulation uniform shoes and the whole uniformed ensemble looked ridiculous and faintly risqué teamed up with our fashionable high heels. My friendship with Beth was sealed during this dressing session and remained a constant throughout our training and beyond – so much so, that our names seemed to be interchangeable and I was frequently referred to as Beth and she as Greta.

Downstairs we went, to the mirth of Miss Cape's subordinates. Miss Davies, who was her deputy, had the misfortune to be the only Sister at Barts who was not Barts-trained. She had, however, been trained at St Thomas's Hospital over the other side of the River Thames, but this was still unforgivable in Miss Cape's eyes, and as the weeks went by we became aware of the antagonism between the two.

Miss Miles, a young Sister with a sweet smile, was wearing an obviously new blue uniform and appeared nervous as she looked at us with sympathy. The final member of the teaching team was the dark-haired, alluringly attractive Miss Allen, a Senior Staff Nurse known as a "Pink" due to her pretty pink, long-sleeved uniform with its smart stiff white collar and cuffs, which, together with her shoulder-length cap, were to be much admired and instantly gave us aspirations of "pink" status.

Miss Allen obviously had a great sense of humour, and she laughed as she viewed our motley crew – some of us in ill-fitting uniforms and others still wearing our soon-to-be-banned make-up, nail varnish and jewellery.

The team of four then lined up to show us how to fashion our caps, and I soon began to wonder why I had so fervently wished to wear one like those I had seen in the Square on the day of my interview. In my three years' of training I never did succeed in making a perfect specimen. 'Fold, pin, pleat and pin again. Fold, pin, pleat and pin again.' We struggled and persevered; to no avail as far as I was concerned.

'Oh no, Nurse Tisdale, *not* like that.'

Next, we were shown a noticeboard on which there were thirty-seven surnames, all of which were prefixed with the letter "N". We all started to say that our first name initial was not "N" until we realised the implication. The "N", we were told, stood for "Nurse", and we were never, *ever*, to use first names when we were on duty.

This was but one of numerous rules at PTS, and it soon became obvious that discipline was a high priority. There were directives regarding laundry, uniform, smoking, baths, ironing, housework and many, many others governing every aspect of our lives and routines. One such was lights out by 10pm. Boyfriends, we were told, were *not* allowed to telephone or to visit us without special permission. If, on the very rare occasion, a visit *was* permitted, the boy could only be seen downstairs. Bedrooms were firmly out of bounds. We were not allowed to wear cosmetics other than face powder to cover a shiny nose. And, last but not least, at the end of a holiday we were to write to Matron saying we were looking forward to returning.

Our weekly pay was to be the grand sum of £2 17s 6d (£2.87), which had to cover essentials such as toiletries and black stockings as well as all our clothes and any travel costs.

Finally, we were informed that a Sister's uniform was not to be referred to as royal blue; it was to be known as *watchett* blue. Apparently, in 1554, the governors of the hospital purchased lengths of watchett blue cloth for the Sisters' liveries, and

Our monthly pay.

over the centuries the Sisters had continued to wear blue; but whilst the hue had changed, the name had not. It was not clear that such details really mattered.

Miss Cape drew herself up to her full height and paused, waiting for silence, before launching into short stories about former matrons which, to her, all had a moral that she clearly felt we needed to take on board before we grew a minute older.

'Margaret Blague,' she said, 'who was the Matron of the hospital during the Great Plague in 1665 remained in her post in London to look after the patients whilst the doctors were too frightened to stay and "desired to be excused to do the service because it was too hot" and they fled to the country.'

MORAL: A GOOD NURSE PUTS DUTY FIRST

'Miss Ethel Manson, appointed Matron in 1881, was required to resign from her post after six years, when she married Dr Gordon Fenwick. Despite this, the indefatigable Miss Manson campaigned for thirty-three years for the state registration of nurses, and when the register finally opened she was listed as Nurse No 1.'

MORAL: WHILST MARRIAGE STILL REQUIRES RESIGNATION FROM THE HOSPITAL, NEVER GIVE UP ON TRYING TO ACHIEVE PERSONAL GOALS

Miss Cape was getting into her stride: 'Isla Stewart, Miss Manson's successor, was responsible for Barts gaining a reputation for being the most progressive of all London hospitals for its nursing policy and training and this continues today.'

MORAL: IT IS A PRIVILEGE TO TRAIN AT ST BARTHOLOMEW'S HOSPITAL

Miss Cape came into her own when she spoke about the awe-inspiring Miss Helen Dey who was appointed Matron and Superintendent of Nurses in 1927 and who became one of the great matrons of the twentieth century.

'Miss Dey's view was that nursing was a vocation to which the professional element was a supplement and she looked for women who were mainly from the middle classes but not from academic backgrounds, as she believed that academics would not do well as nurses.'

MORAL: BEING CLEVER DOESN'T
EQUATE TO EXCELLENCE

Miss Cape had had her say, and we mere students exchanged surreptitious glances, but we were duly impressed and ready to do our bit.

Our first day was at last drawing to a close and Beth and I welcomed our sleep, and were tucked up by 9.30pm in readiness for our curfew. Before settling down, I sat, propped up in bed by a bulky pillow, and reached for my new red page-a-day 1959 diary. This was a gift from my father to encourage me to write a Hospital Journal about events and experiences during my training, with his promise to provide me with new diaries in successive years. I filled my fountain pen from a bottle of Royal Blue Quink and began to write – *Started at Barts.* Soon, the page filled with neat blue writing.

Chapter Three

The Correct Way of Doing Things

Life during our ten weeks at Piggotts Manor was very full. Housework was our first duty of the day – there were few domestic staff and the Sisters were very particular, especially Miss Davies from St Thomas's who was in charge of our cleaning rota. She began our first cleaning session with: 'Nurses, I want you to listen very carefully. There is a correct way of doing everything whether you are damp dusting, dry dusting, sweeping the floor, cleaning basins or polishing the brass taps on the baths. It is not only important to stand back and be critical of your endeavours, but also to take pleasure in the results of the task you have completed, however menial. Leave the place always as you would wish to find it. Do you understand?' We nodded politely but didn't see how all this housework had any bearing on nursing the sick.

Miss Miles, the new girl in blue, took the practical cookery classes and was infinitely patient. She showed us how to cut paper-thin bread and how to present it, buttered, with the crusts cut off and served in triangles, so it would appeal to a sick patient. We were taught how to boil the perfect egg and how not to overdo the scrambled variety; how to cook steamed fish to perfection as well as other tempting, nourishing delicacies including junket, which was a pudding made of sweetened and flavoured curds of milk and had the appearance of sour milk. It was considered easy for the patients to swallow, but I personally felt its slimy consistency was entirely unpalatable.

One day, Miss Miles took a deep breath. 'Now I need to tell you the most important rule of all.' We waited expectantly. '*Everything* you carry, from a complete meal to a glass of water, or even a single teaspoon, must *always* be transported to the patient on a tray.'

Did this mean, having delivered an item to the patient, we had to retrace our steps with an empty tray back to the ward kitchen, we asked. 'Most certainly and never, ever, leave unfinished food in front of the patient. Get a tray and clear the locker immediately,' was the answer.

The worst day of all for me at PTS was when we had to sew laundry marks on to all our uniform, including the stiff buckram belts, as well as any other garments we wished to send to the laundry. My number was 712, and it will be etched in my memory forever. I was no seamstress, having achieved only fourteen per cent in a needlework exam, and I pricked my finger countless times and managed to "bloody" several items as I stitched. To make matters worse, we had to embroider our name in black embroidery silk

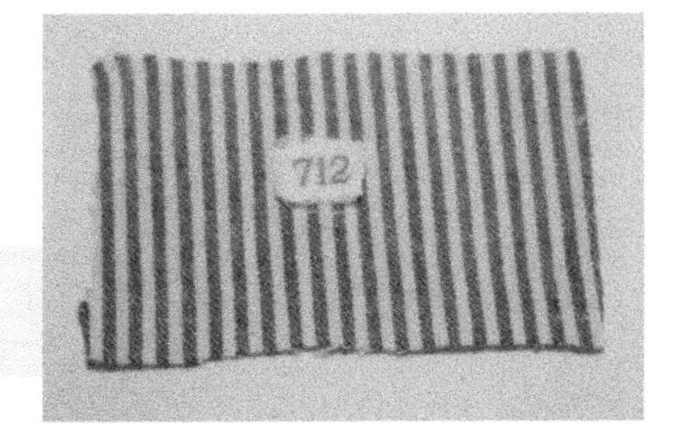

The number 712 was never to be forgotten.

on the red inside of our capes – mine looked abysmal. I made the decision there and then that come what may, I was going to complete the next three years and I would not let these hours go to waste.

Learning how to make the various types of hospital bed was more to my liking. Making a straightforward bed with hospital corners had to be synchronised and completed by two nurses within three minutes so the patient was disturbed as little as possible. The sheets had to be tucked under the mattress simultaneously and the mitring (corners) carried out to perfection. The open ends of the pillows always had to be placed facing down the room, away from the door, to present a tidy appearance, and the four wheels of the bed had to face inwards, arranged in an orderly fashion. We were reminded firmly that when we were making beds it should be seen as an opportunity to talk to the patient, provided they were well enough (and that if they were too ill they would require our undivided attention) – in other words, bed-making should *not* be seen as an opportunity to talk to the other nurse.

There were an overwhelming number of "special beds" which we had to learn, and remember how to make; there was the closed bed for non-specialised cases; the admission bed for emergency cases which had to include an electric blanket and two old, laundered blankets so patients in street clothes could be put into bed without soiling the sheets; various fracture beds – including the divided and envelope types, some requiring a fracture board to be laid beneath the mattress. There were amputation beds, acute heart failure beds as well as the chronic heart failure variety and post-operation beds; the list went on and on. Naturally, apple-pie beds were not part of the curriculum; and anyway, we were already acquainted with this childish prank.

I was instructed to make a simple "closed" bed with a

partner. We were both very satisfied with our efforts, having remembered to turn over the mattress and to lift it close to the top rail of the bed, to put on the long mackintosh, the bottom sheet, the short mackintosh, the draw sheet, the top sheet and finally a beautifully mitred blanket; as a final touch the counterpane was put in place with aplomb and the pillows positioned with precision and the four wheels of the bed turned inwards.

Judgement time arrived.

'Nurses; this is just not good enough.'

We had just spent five minutes admiring our handiwork and were now utterly perplexed.

'Nurses, use your eyes!'

We did as instructed and were still none the wiser.

'Look at the counterpane.'

It looked perfect to us, but apparently we had put the blue and beige woven counterpane on the bed inside out, even though to our blinkered eyes it had appeared entirely reversible.

Of course, our ineptitude at this stage ensured that we were not introduced to real patients. Instead, we had two dummies, affectionately known as Victoria and Angelina, on whom we learnt and practised various techniques and procedures. They were limp and life-sized and extraordinarily difficult to handle, but they endured our over-zealous handling with magnanimity. And if we should dare to treat them with disrespect or irreverence, we were soon shown the error of our ways by our tutors. Miss Cape and Miss Davies demonstrated procedures talking earnestly to the "patient" all the while, and we just tried to hide our mirth. When it was our turn, Beth – who always looked as though butter wouldn't melt in her mouth – excelled. 'Blast your silly legs; I can't tuck the sheet in' or 'Why won't you bend your arm so I can put this wretched bandage on?' She always managed to carry out these one-sided conversations with a sympathetic air, and out of hearing of the tutors, but always within our range of enjoyment.

We couldn't believe the number of items required to carry out a simple bed bath for our lovely ladies, but most of all it was Miss Cape's voice of experience that was never to be forgotten. 'Don't forget all the creases!' she cried. 'Lift the breast up and wash and dry well before dusting with talcum powder!' 'Massage the buttocks to prevent bed sores!' 'Hand the patient a fresh flannel so she can attend to her own genitalia.'

We soon learnt the value of modesty and comfort as we, too, suffered the indignity and ministrations of our fellow students. We bandaged each other from top to toe – spirals, figures of 8, capelines (which were particularly tricky as two roller bandages had to be wound round the head at the same time) and "T" bandages, as well as the many-tailed bandage, which required hand sewing and was, of course, not to my liking. Luckily, we did manage to avoid giving each other the dreaded enema.

Our nursing "family" was completed by Jimmy and Fred, the human skeletons who lived in the practical room, dangling from hooks. It was intended that we should learn the names of all the bones of the body from these delightful gentlemen, but as far as I can remember, none of us succeeded. However, one night Jimmy – or it could have been Fred – was kidnapped and found in the bathroom where he had been plonked on the lavatory. In the middle of the night, a poor unsuspecting girl had the shock of her life when responding to the call of nature; she ended up sitting on his knee. Her piercing screams woke us all and Miss Davies was soon briskly on the scene. The rogue was swiftly

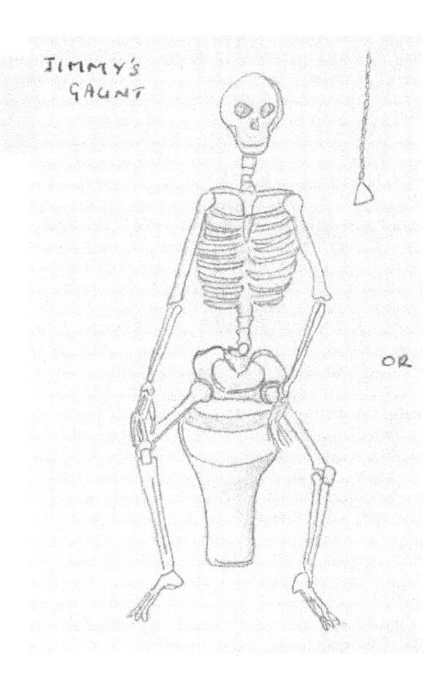

Jimmy, drawn by Beth, enjoyed his night time joke.

returned to his rightful place and he never disclosed who had helped him in the jape. We conspirators just smiled. Our lips were sealed.

We enjoyed learning how to lay up trolleys for different medical and surgical procedures, although these lessons did strike home the seriousness of the roles we were to take on. I was certainly relieved to learn that sending for medical assistance in the case of emergencies was as crucial as carrying out primary first aid.

The necessary academic side of nursing was well covered and included lectures on anatomy, physiology and hygiene which were tolerated, but not received with great enthusiasm by most of us. Much more interesting, as far as I was concerned, were the basic principles for various diseases requiring special nursing – these, I felt, were of greater relevance to the care of the patient.

Jackie, a lovely but scatty girl, put up her hand each time illnesses were mentioned to ask whether she could "catch it". The question always caused laughter among us students, but it didn't go down at all well with the tutors. Jackie was fated from the first day when she dropped a full bottle of royal blue ink on a large area of parquet floor shortly after being told there was to be no ink in the classroom. Next, she sat through a deck chair and by the third day, when we had a group photograph taken, it was noted her collar was held on by numerous safety pins. This wasn't all; she had mistakenly sewn her laundry numbers on the wrong side of all her aprons and had to unpick them all and do a re-sew. She had lost books, missed lectures and was always forgetting things. Perhaps her greatest sin in the eyes of the tutors, though, was when she and a fellow student each bought a conspicuously new Lambretta from Watford. The brave, or possibly mad, girls had never sat on a scooter before, let alone driven one. Nevertheless, they proudly arrived back at Piggotts Manor relatively unscathed and quite confident, until Jackie took one of her hands off the handlebar to give us a heroic wave before landing in a beautifully maintained hedge, to the disgust of the gardener. She kept offering us a ride but we valued our lives and declined.

Jackie was never going to comply with nursing etiquette, which was considered of the utmost importance. We were told we should: 'Stand up when addressing your seniors, open doors and stand aside to allow people to pass and be professional at all times but particularly in front of patients.' Good manners were everything. We were also informed that there was a Nursing Code which was threefold: *To conserve life, to alleviate suffering and to promote health* – all of which seemed to me to be entirely appropriate, but did we need so many rules?

If we were ever fortunate enough to hold a conversation with a consultant surgeon or physician, we were informed they were *always* to be addressed as "Sir". I had cause to put this new-found etiquette into practice when Professor Garrod came to perform Schick tests on us all to check whether we were already immune to diphtheria. We lined up in silence as Miss Cape checked our uniforms for perfection and were then called in one by one to see the great man. Miss Cape kept a close eye on the procedure and was "Sir'ing" the professor all over the place as she enthusiastically bobbed up and down. Emulating Miss

Cape, I managed a timid 'Thank you, sir', as I carried out a mild bob with embarrassment.

Physical education classes were held weekly by a hearty instructor who forced us to undertake cross-country running to aid our endurance and stamina and in preparation for the future long hours of duty on the wards. The classes didn't go down too well, and we all behaved in a very un-ladylike manner, kitted out in a mix of old school shorts and aertex shirts. It was during these gruelling sessions that we were ordered to lie on our backs with our bare feet in the air so that the Sister Tutor could check for athlete's foot – the "culprits" had to have their toes painted with a bright gentian violet solution.

Our education was completed by visits to the local waterworks and to the sewage station, about which I remember very little, apart from the smell. We couldn't see the point of these outings, but they were obligatory, so that was the end of it.

We got to know each other well at PTS and the value of belonging to a specific "set" undoubtedly paid off. It was evident that some girls already had close links to the hospital. A number of their fathers were Barts-trained doctors and their mothers were Barts-trained nurses – maybe those romantic library books at Letchmore Heath weren't far off the mark. Nursing was still very much seen as a female occupation which was chiefly to provide care and nurture to the patient. Medicine was for men and few women aspired to be doctors. Undoubtedly, even the physician father still saw his daughter in the female role even if she had the academic qualifications, as many of us did, to study medicine. Little had changed since 1888 when the distinguished Barts physician Sir Dyce Duckworth – who supported the new breed of lady probationer nurses by becoming vice president of the newly formed Royal British Nurses Association – declared that the public did not understand the position of a well-educated trained nurse. However, he told a gathering of probationer nurses in 1895 that their job was to carry out the doctor's orders with implicit obedience and exactitude; and if a nurse had any opinions she should keep them to herself. This traditionalist couldn't imagine that any decent woman would wish to study medicine and maintained that the proper place for women was at home or, at most, as nurses.

In our group there were a couple of older students. Barbara was a twenty-three-year-old anaemic-looking Scots girl, who was fortunate in being allocated a single room because of her great age, whilst Gayle was a rebel who was frightened of no one and thought nothing of speaking her mind. Jane, who was not only clever but was an obvious leader, became our "head girl" and was voted unanimously to be our set representative. Dark-haired Paula with her rosy cheeks and deep brown eyes was the beauty of the set and was to break many hearts.

Six individuals became my closest friends. There was my roommate Beth, whose father was a professor of veterinary medicine at the University of Bristol; and pretty, wavy-haired Meg who had an attractive gap between her front teeth, who was the daughter of a London solicitor. These two appeared to have come straight out of Louisa May Alcott's much-loved book *Little Women*. Tall and willowy Priscilla was one of six children and was the daughter of a surgeon who had worked in the mission field. Anna, yet another doctor's daughter, was Polish but had been

Head girl Jane, back row extreme left, Beth back row 4th in, next to Priscilla. Meg kneeling left, next to Greta.

brought up in Scotland where she had acquired a charming soft Scottish accent, and became well known for her penchant for expensive shoes. Anne was a farmer's daughter who we all thought was rather quiet and meek until she taught us how to hitchhike. I seem to remember we had a placard on which we plastered the word NURSES; it worked wonders as we never failed to get a lift. I didn't tell my parents of our colourful exploits, but as we never travelled alone, we felt there was safety in numbers. Finally, there was the exuberant, fresh-faced Mary from Derby, who had the most explosive and infectious laugh imaginable.

We all worked hard – apart from Beth who was particularly clever and tended to write poetry rather than study – but this didn't stop us from having a great deal of fun. However, all too often a party or even a late-night chat had barely begun before it was discovered. Beth and I decided to celebrate Meg's birthday by putting on a cabaret. We had no fancy dress, and so improvisation was required. I was decked out in a fur hat, a papery stiff crinoline petticoat (masquerading as a strapless dress), long red socks and white high heels. Beth captured the hilarity of the evening in her tattered pyjama bottoms, a bikini top, a dressing gown cord tied round her head and her beloved bell rope wound round her waist, accessorised with multiple bangles. We hijacked Barbara's single room, who was unaware

My make-shift fancy dress drawn by Beth.

we had even planned the event. She was ready for bed, robed in a black negligée, pins in her hair and with a white face pack in position. Ten of us invaded her room and were ready to have fun – fuelled by lemonade alone as alcohol was firmly forbidden – when mid-cabaret, Beth and I were stopped in full swing. Miss Davies appeared in her sensible dressing gown and hair net, and although she roared with laughter at the pair of us in our resplendent costumes, this didn't stop her immediately packing us all off to bed.

Frequently, even if we were just chatting quietly, usually about romance or religion, Miss Davies would appear in her nightwear minutes after the curfew, with a firm reminder: 'Nurse Tisdale, it's already 10.45. You will never pass your exams or make a responsible nurse if you do not abide by the rules.' My name must have been embedded in her brain for it felt as though I was always the one she singled out.

Miss Davies was not my only nemesis. I also found myself in hot water with Miss Cape and on one occasion was summoned to her office. 'Nurse Tisdale, I have to speak to you on two accounts. Firstly, I'm aware you received a bouquet of red carnations this morning. Am I correct?' I nodded shamefully. 'Then, a gentleman called Walter telephoned this afternoon and asked to speak to you. How he found our number I don't know as we are ex-directory, but regardless, you know full well this is not allowed. I cannot have you being distracted by the opposite sex.'

I was mortified. The "giver" of the bouquet, a fellow member of our local tennis club, may have been a dark-haired, blue-eyed Adonis, but he was not for me. The "gentleman" sleuth was a different matter. He was, indeed, called Walter and was a schoolmaster who taught French. He wasn't handsome; he had a flattened, crooked nose due to skirmishes on the rugby pitch; and to crown it all, he was half French and already twenty-eight years old. We had met on holiday in France three years previously when he had shown me the glorious Provencal countryside in his open-topped old banger called *Sylvette*. The never-ending sea of intoxicating purple lavender had provided a romantic backdrop to our excursions. Still, in spite of his rugby credentials, Walter was a gentle giant and had not taken advantage of my youth, and there had been nothing more than a friendly embrace.

After giving me my dressing-down, Miss Cape looked me in the eye and, to give her her due, she smiled, gave me a nudge and came out with her favourite phrase: 'See what I mean?'

My journal entry that evening read:

> *I can't believe it! Walter somehow managed to obtain the telephone number of the PTS. I was so embarrassed. I've just spoken to him and told him this wasn't allowed and he mustn't ring again and that I thought it wasn't advisable to go out with a male acquaintance whilst I was here.*

There was no doubt we were undeniably governed by rules, and most of us, somewhat surprisingly, abided by them.

Chapter Four

To Fleet Street

May 25th was a Red Letter Day. We were told on which ward we had been allocated at Barts for the start of our nursing duties, and the one chosen would be the one on which we would spend our first three months as a "pro" (probationer). This day, though, was just the first of three planned ward visits where each time our hours on the ward would be increased. Poor Meg was going to Hill End in St Albans, the branch hospital of Barts, which she found very upsetting as this was in her home town and she was desperate to get to London to start her new life. I was allocated to work on Fleet Street, a male surgical ward; this was good news as I was sure that men were going to be more fun to nurse than Victoria and Angelina had proved to be. My excitement knew no bounds, and I could hardly wait for the momentous event.

The coach arrived to take us up to the City of London and off we went. Shoes polished, clean dresses, sparkling aprons (with a spare in case of accidents) and our caps pleated to perfection – we were determined to show ourselves at our best.

As I entered the long, clean and tidy ward I was aware that this was the moment for which I had been waiting since my childhood days with Bertie the bear as my prize patient. Now, at last, I was going to nurse real live patients.

The ward was of the Nightingale type and was one large room divided by a partition down the middle, leaving room for Sister's desk at the entrance, allowing her to observe all her patients at any one time. There were twenty-four beds in total in the main ward with an additional two side rooms. As I walked towards my goal, I could see a sluice room, a kitchen and a laundry room, and on my arrival I noticed instantly an immaculate ward with all the wheels of the beds turned to face inwards and every pillowcase with its opening facing away from the ward door. Miss Cape would have been pleased. All the men were in bed having their afternoon rest. Peace reigned.

My contribution on this visit was simply to serve tea, but the reward for my modest service was immense. All the patients gratefully said, 'Thank you, Nurse,' and I couldn't have wished for more.

One of the men was a journalist. He spotted immediately that I was a new nurse, and he was eager to tell me the origin of the ward's name. Apparently, Fleet Street journalists were great supporters of Barts and used to refer to the hospital as "the Mother Hospital of the Empire". In 1926, the journalists raised a huge sum of money by organising an event called Fleet Street Week for Barts, and by 1927, they were able to hand over a cheque for an amazing £25,000 for the Reconstruction Fund of the hospital. This was on condition that one of the wards would be called Fleet Street. The request was granted, and I could see why the patient was keen to tell me the tale. Here I was, thirty years later, likely to be nursing many patients from the world of printing and journalism.

On my second visit to the hospital, I thought I was ready for anything. I was allowed to bed bath a patient, to prepare

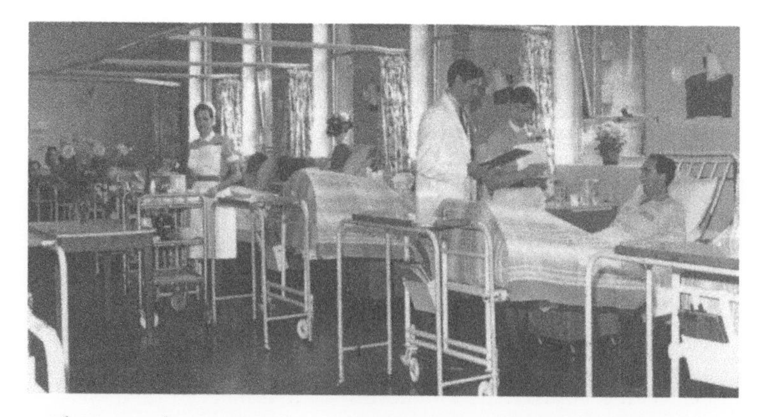

Fleet Street Ward named in recognition of the support provided by the Fleet Street journalists.

and serve the teas, to make numerous beds, "do a back" (a term used euphemistically for rubbing a patient's bottom with surgical spirit and then talcum powder to prevent bed sores) and to measure some urine. I was told by Miss Davies, who had been hovering over me like a mother hen, to report to Sister Fleet Street, the Ward Sister.

This turned out to be a big mistake. 'Go away, you silly girl. I'm much too busy to see you.' I knew that defending myself was not an option, so I left the ward without a murmur, but I felt a great injustice had been done.

My third visit to the hospital was for the whole day, so the alarm clock was set for 6am that morning as we had to complete our household duties before breakfast. It was full speed ahead with the duster, and then off to Aldenham Cottage for bacon, tomato, toast and marmalade, and a quick cup of tea to swill it all down. We all got the jitters on the way up to the hospital; however, mine soon vanished when I got on to the ward where I started to feel as though I, almost, belonged.

This didn't last. Within a couple of minutes a houseman (a newly qualified doctor) came from behind a curtained bed, his hands dripping with blood. 'Scissors, Nurse, scissors,' he demanded. *Scissors, scissors*?

For a moment, I couldn't even think what scissors were. As luck would have it, I instinctively went to the top pocket of my uniform dress and produced my scissors. So far, so good. Then he asked me to cut some sticking plaster for him. Where should I cut it? Near the barrel? In the middle? At the end? We were taught precisely how to do procedures in the classroom, so I felt there must be a correct place. Anyway, I compromised by cutting it between the barrel and the middle. He didn't complain.

Next came lunch duties – a major and important part of the day. Every patient had a polished wooden locker on which was laid a crisp white cotton cloth, edged in green. Sister served the food at twelve noon sharp. She carefully wiped round each plate for any spills as the nurses stood in a queue to take the first course – on a tray, of course – to the patients. I noticed that all the patients who needed feeding were fed unhurriedly by a nurse sitting at the patient's bedside. Pudding was served once the main course plates had been cleared.

We were allowed half an hour for our lunch which was held in the Nurses' Dining Room, but I was told that if we ever got off duty late for lunch, we still had to be back on duty within the allocated half an hour. I enjoyed delicious soup, which was followed by lamb and potatoes, or steak and kidney pie, or salad. *Three* choices. To follow was sago or gooseberries and custard, and then cheese and biscuits and finally a cup of tea. The hum of chatter in the room never ceased.

Gayle told us she was already in hot water. After her last visit to her designated ward, she had asked Miss Cape whether it was necessary to have a cover on an inhaler as there had not been one on the inhaler she had been told to give to a patient. Subsequently, our senior Sister Tutor wrote a very accusing letter to the Ward Sister who in turn was furious with the nurses, who swore black and blue they had used a cover; and they, of course, were extremely cross with Gayle who said she had only been asking a simple question.

A conducted tour of a spotless operating theatre and sterilising room was next on the agenda, and then it was back to the ward for more duties before returning to Piggotts Manor, exhausted but happy.

After ten weeks of camaraderie, fun and almost unbroken sunshine, the dreaded PTS exams arrived. I was fortunate in being exempt from taking the anatomy and physiology paper as I had passed 'O' level human biology. I felt just a twinge of guilt at my good fortune but have to admit I didn't spend too much time sympathising with my less fortunate fellow students. The oral examination was conducted by the redoubtable Miss Hector, the Principal Sister Tutor at Barts. If this wasn't daunting enough, the practical exam was overseen by an Assistant Matron who watched our every move in order to mark down our faults and, as Beth commented, with any luck, perhaps all our virtues.

The first question on the written paper gave us much cause for concern, as it was on the retention of urine – a topic we had yet to cover. We exchanged furtive glances, and it was only when Head Girl Jane raised the alarm that the invigilator contacted the Nursing School at Barts and the question was changed. This time it was on sterilisation: how to sterilise a dressing packet; a monometal bowl; a gum elastic catheter and a glass funnel. This was straightforward, but nonetheless important, as the new Central Sterilisation Unit was yet to be introduced at the hospital and these tasks would be our responsibility.

We were asked to describe how to care for a sick patient's mouth and to give reasons for carrying out the procedure. Finally, notes had to be written on a rigor (sudden shivering with a raised temperature), Cheyne-Stokes Respirations (an interrupted pattern of breathing, sometimes called the "death rattle"), pyrexia (raised body temperature leading to a fever) and tachycardia (an abnormally rapid heartbeat).

The final exam was on first aid: we were given two emergency situations and asked how we would deal with them. The first was that of an elderly lady seen in a bus queue bleeding from her leg, potentially due to varicose veins, and the second was a boy who fainted in a street watching a procession go by. Both questions, we decided, required more common sense than nursing expertise.

The exams were over, but our anxiety about the results was made worse by Miss Cape's announcement: 'Those of you who fail the examination, whether it be the written papers, the oral, or the practical and have therefore not made the grade during your time at PTS will be asked to leave immediately.'

The atmosphere was tense, but we had a day or so before our results were due, and our nerves were put to one side when we were invited to attend a garden party for disabled First World War veterans from the Star and Garter Home in Richmond. Their time during the war was still so fresh in their memory, and they told us of the singing and the whistling of the song *Tipperary*, foot rot in the trenches and the loss of friends during the Battle of the Somme. Although many had been badly injured, the veterans were in good heart. The afternoon had been inspirational and had

Greta & Beth putting on a brave face as they wait for their exam results.

left an everlasting impression on me. Suddenly, the passing, or even the failing, of my exam paled into insignificance.

However, the nerves were still there when decision day arrived. We spent the morning spring cleaning Piggotts Manor. I was tasked with turning out what seemed like hundreds of already completely clean cupboards. Nevertheless, I re-scrubbed all the shelves and made sure that all the labels on the bottles faced to the front and were in neat rows starting from the biggest at the back to the smallest at the front – a habit which to this day I cannot break.

At last, Miss Cape pinned up the results on the notice board. With the exception of poor Annette the Welsh girl, who was a loner and whom none of us had got to know well, we had all passed. Her news overshadowed our joy but by the evening, we had cheered up and we let our hair down by having our usual alcohol-free party. The theme this time was to dress up as an anatomical name. Ingenuity was the order of the day and we "purloined" bedspreads, sheets, wastepaper baskets and rugs from Piggotts, as well as using our own uniforms, bathing costumes and nightdresses. The Sisters were asked to be judges, and the contestants included two Roman Gladiators clothed in bedspread togas named *Os calcis* and *Astragulus*. Beth won the competition representing "the Left Bank of the Islets of Langerhans", kitted out in a bikini and black stockings.

None of us knew what lay ahead, but we agreed we would always have the ten weeks to look back on, and we had had the happiest of all beginnings. Now we were on our way.

Chapter Five

A Pro at Last

After a well-deserved week's holiday, we arrived at Barts on 21st July, revived and refreshed. Our first duty was to report to the Home Sister's office, where we had to sign a statement undertaking that we would not enter the medical residences. This was known as "signing the pledge" – after which we all immediately enquired as to the whereabouts of these attractive residences.

We came to know the Home Sister, Miss Dye, only too well over the years, but on our arrival she was merely our hostess. She showed us around the rather grand-sounding Queen Mary's Nurses' Home which was huge, ugly and imposing and felt very intimidating in comparison with the gracious and homely Piggotts Manor. It had an abundance of long, dark corridors with floors covered in the customary dark brown linoleum, which squeaked continuously from the friction of our rubber-soled uniform shoes as we scurried along behind Miss Dye.

The brisk tour did, however, bring some pleasurable surprises, including two attractive nurses' sitting rooms. The

The large Nurses' Sitting Room where fresh flowers were always in evidence.

largest of these was quite baronial and had polished solid oak flooring with a large, fringed multi-coloured rug as its focus. Completing the furnishings were an upright piano, several standard and table lamps, and an array of chintz-covered sofas and arm chairs. An artistic arrangement of fresh flowers had been placed on a round antique oak table. I remembered this room only too well; it was the one in which I had danced the *Gay Gordons* when I attended the hospital to see the neurologist and where Nurse Downton had strongly advised me not to take up nursing. I was quite relieved to move on to the smaller of the two sitting rooms, which was less formal and seemed to invite the giving of confidences.

Next was the Isla Stewart Reference Library, which housed an impressive collection of publications and books. This orderly, pine-panelled room of academia did not appear to be well used, and the books were securely locked away in their glass-fronted bookcases. Apart from the portrait above the mantelpiece of

The Isla Stewart Reference Library had a feel of academia.

Miss Isla Stewart, the progressive and renowned Barts matron whose reign had extended from 1887 to 1910, the library could have been mistaken for the smoking room of a gentlemen's club with its deep, masculine, leather arm chairs. I liked the room, though, and its air of respectability and solidarity.

The Nurses' Hairdressing Salon was quite another story. Its grand title belied its shabbiness, but apparently it served its purpose well; and the hairdresser, we were told, did a very reasonably priced shampoo and set. Surprisingly, the hospital had its own branch of the National Provincial Bank, today known as Nat West, and as far as I can remember, we all "joined" there and then.

We were each allocated a single room on the sixth floor of the Nurses' Home. When we were introduced to our new accommodation, we were horrified. The rooms were tiny; and by tiny, I mean *really* tiny; there was space, just, for a narrow single bed, a small built-in wardrobe and a chair. What little there was

"Perms" and "sets" were popular in the Hair Salon.

left of the floor was, once again, covered in brown linoleum. The communal bathroom was situated a long way down the windowless corridor from my room. There were no showers and just a few huge claw-footed baths.

Still, there was some welcome and rather unexpected news. We had two lovely maids to whom we were introduced. One was called Maud and the other Amelia and both came from Jamaica. One was big and black and the other thin and black; they were absolute treasures and were never without a smile. We loved them. Maud said with pride, 'Our job is to clean your rooms, make your beds and bring you your breakfast in bed twice a month.' What a treat.

As we left Maud and Amelia to go to our first supper, we missed Meg and thought about her having to work at the run-down hospital in St Albans. Beth, Priscilla, Mary, Anna, Anne and I went into the Nurses' Dining Room where we sat at an empty table. This was not a good idea, as we soon found out. New probationers were meant to sit in the lowliest position in the dining room, but nobody had told us this and we had blithely taken our seats among our superiors. Shamefacedly, we moved and never made the same mistake again.

There were other rules, too. We were told the curfew was 10.30pm but that we could have two late passes a week until midnight, signed by the Ward Sister, and in very exceptional cases an extended late pass until 2.30am could be obtained from Matron. We learnt at the same time that having a ladder in your stocking was considered a major misdemeanour and had to be rectified instantly. There was also an intriguing regulation. We had to take our capes off, even if it was midwinter and we were outdoors, whenever we passed a Sister Tutor; the all-enveloping navy overgarment, with its comforting red lining, had to be flung back across the shoulders, leaving us to shiver in our short-sleeved cotton dresses until "her majesty" had metaphorically raised her arm graciously and moved on. We never understood exactly when or why this tradition came to be.

As I prepared for bed that first night and settled into my humble abode, I felt happy. At last the years of waiting were over. I was a real pro.

*

The clanging of a hand bell, reminiscent of our schooldays, woke us at 6.20am. Creating this incessant noise was obviously giving a degree of sadistic enjoyment to the ringer as she woke others from their slumber. It was an awful awakening and one that I never got used to. The bell ringer marched up and down all the corridors, and we were told that it was rung at this time every morning, regardless of whether the sleeping nurses were going on duty or not.

After the bell-ringing and a quick strip wash, Beth and I felt in need of spiritual refreshment, so we went to 7am Communion at St Bartholomew the Less. The little church was the only survivor of other medieval chapels belonging to the hospital and had been on its present site since 1184. When Henry VIII refounded the hospital in 1546, its precinct was established as the Anglican parish of St Bartholomew the Less, and it became unique among English hospitals as a parish in its own right. Until the nineteenth century, it was compulsory for nursing staff, and patients who were fit enough, to attend church services. In 1682,

The church of St Bartholomew the Less.

the governors were asked to check whether they and all in their employ were attending Communion according to the rites of the Church of England. This put the cat among the pigeons, as it was found that the brewer, baker, ironmonger, turner, mason, tinman, flaxman, mealman and stationer all had to be dismissed for non-attendance! For some of us, the church became very special as a place of peaceful refuge over the years, particularly in times of distress, which were unavoidable in daily hospital life. There were quite a number of Sisters in the congregation that morning; and as time went by, it became apparent that for many of them, religion played a major role in their nursing vocation.

After an obligatory blood test and a chest X-ray, I reported at 1.30pm for duty on Fleet Street Ward and worked until 8pm. Day duty hours were forty-nine hours a week with one whole day off a week that was always preceded by an evening off. Nurse Downton had been right those many months ago – by the time I came off duty, my feet *were* killing me. Forty-nine hours a *week*.

Two days after starting on the ward, I felt as though I was going to collapse from exhaustion. Although we had three hours off during the day, the days were nearly twelve hours long. My duties were menial but nonetheless necessary. That particular day, on which I nearly reached the end of my reserves, I had distributed numerous bedpans and bottles and post-operative inhalers, and had rubbed backs and bottoms, cleaned lockers, carbolised three beds and three mattresses, and taken the TPR (temperature, pulse and respiration rate) of all twenty-six patients on the ward. I had also spent time carrying out the important task of mouth care, including brushing the teeth of those patients who required special treatment to keep their mouths and tongues clean and were unable to do it for themselves. Throughout the day, I had made "hundreds" of beds with the all-important wheels turned in and with the openings of pillowcases facing away from the door and, of course, the cockleshell pattern on the counterpanes the right way up. I had buttered bread with great difficulty because the butter was rock hard but became too soft when I melted it under the grill, and I had served tea from a large teapot to the patients and transported meals (always on a tray), which had been beautifully served by Sister. My final task was to remove all the flowers from the ward into the sluice to remain there overnight as the carbon dioxide they gave off in the dark was considered harmful.

As if all this wasn't enough, a second-year nurse came up to me and said, 'I'm just going through.'

I wasn't too happy to be left on the ward without her support after only a couple of days and respectfully I asked, 'Where are you going "through to"?'

She laughed and replied, 'You'll soon get used to everyone saying it; it's another way of saying you are going to the lavatory. It comes from the time when Sisters used to sleep on the ward and they went "through" from their room to the ward bathroom.' She went on, 'Another Barts phrase is "Have you had one for the book?": a question we ask daily of every patient to check if they have opened their bowels.' Another lesson learnt.

The next day, I woke refreshed. We had all followed the "bed on the laundry basket" recommendation, where the bottom of the bed was lifted onto the top of the basket so the sleeper's legs and feet were higher than the rest of the body. It did the trick for me. Others, I believe, tried the "bottom on the floor with your legs at a right angle going up the wall" technique. The only problem with this method was that it had to be implemented in the corridor because there wasn't enough room to carry out the manoeuvre in the bedroom.

As the days passed, I began to feel less of a spare part and started to enjoy working in a team. On the weekends, I had extra domestic duties and was responsible for vacuuming the ward and cleaning and polishing all the patients' lockers. Although these tasks were not very significant, they made a considerable difference to my happiness and well-being on a Monday morning. The problem was not so much the tasks in themselves, but Milly the demon ward maid who was a cockney of the not-so-cheery kind and had worked at the hospital for years. She was well into her fifties, and her dyed red hair sprang forth from its grey roots. Milly thought she was second-in-command to Sister on the ward, and I, and many others, considered she was too. I remained in healthy awe of her fiery reputation as she checked my cleaning prowess by looking under the beds for fluff and dust. If she found even a smidgen of dirt, she threatened to report the crime to Sister.

Apart from Milly, life was good on Fleet Street. I learnt much under Sister's watchful eye. And *watch* she did. Whether it was the first time I proudly gave an enema or the occasion when I first removed a patient's stitches and the patient bravely said it didn't hurt at all – I felt I was starting to emerge as a real nurse. Then the day came when I gave my first injection. My patient on this occasion was a white-haired gentleman called Mr Passingham who was very jaundiced. His yellow skin was soft and smooth, and as I prepared the glass syringe and attached a needle to its nozzle, my hand was shaking and I kept muttering to myself 'Upper outer quadrant' as the patient lay on his left side hoping the "dart" would be on target. 'Upper outer quadrant, upper outer quadrant,' I mumbled. I drew an imaginary line with my forefinger over his right buttock, dividing it into quarters. 'Here we go,' I breezed cheerily to him, trying to reassure myself at the same time. The needle went in like a dream and Mr Passingham seemed quite happy, whilst I, on the other hand, definitely felt light-headed.

One of my more tricky duties was cutting old men's toenails. This was no easy task as many of the nails were thick and horny like prehistoric monsters' claws. Almost without exception, though, these often unkempt old men maintained a barrage of witty banter that made them a joy to nurse.

The *young* men's cheek wasn't bad either. On one occasion, shortly after I had started on the ward, twenty-five-year-old Vinnie, who was a very bad burns case, was on the list for a bed bath. I collected all the items required, pulled the curtains round his bed and started washing him in the professional manner in which I had been so well instructed. Suddenly Vinnie said in a very loud voice, 'Oh, Nurse, stop it! Stop it, I tell you!' and then, 'Ah, do it again!' I leapt speedily out of the cubicle, complete with flannel in hand and a very red face. A voice came from behind the curtain, 'You chaps all owe me half a crown. I told you I could make the new nurse blush.' It was just as well Sister wasn't around.

I thought I was doing really quite well on the ward until I was summoned to Sister's room. I had not seen it before, and I was surprised to see that it was furnished as a pleasant sitting room rather than, as I had expected, a bleak office. Needless to say, I was not being called to her room for a friendly chat. I was in trouble. Sister Fleet Street admonished me for being too extravagant with the tea and sugar. I was told in no uncertain terms to be more economical, and my cup of joy was summarily overturned.

The kitchen and the sluice were the junior pro's domain. When I wasn't being extravagant with the tea and coffee or clearing away in the kitchen, I was emptying and measuring urine, vomit or sputum in the sluice. It was whilst performing such functions that I was invited to go out for coffee by a junior house doctor. It turned out that the sluice was deemed the perfect private rendezvous for such invitations. I declined – it would have just been too embarrassing.

A number of patients were nursed on Fleet Street Ward until they died; many had cancer but were not told of their diagnosis and were unaware they had the disease. In the 1950s, the word cancer struck even greater fear in people's hearts than today, as it nearly always heralded certain death. I noted in my journal that I thought it was *a good thing they are none the wiser.* As a raw eighteen-year-old, I found it difficult to cope with the thought of people dying but inevitably had to face it. One of the first times I had to face this reality was when I nursed young Joe Rossi, a fourteen-year-old with cancer of the scrotum who walked around the ward wearing the hospital's regulation towelling dressing gown chatting to anyone he could find. He was adored by his parents, and although they were not wealthy, they had bought him all the gifts he desired, including an expensive watch which he delighted in showing everyone. Joe was able to go home for a few brief months, but he was admitted back to Fleet Street Ward in November as he became sicker, by which time I had moved to a different ward; but I kept in touch with how he was doing. He died on the evening of 6th December at 11.35pm. I could hardly bear to note the event in my journal that night:

> *Dear Joe Rossi died this evening. It's so hard to believe; he was so full of life and was always looking to the future. I met his parents as they were walking across the Square on their way home; they looked so tired and worn out. How*

terrible it must be to lose a child. It seems that everyone at the hospital knew of Joe and his bravery and cheerfulness. Although we have been taught not to show any emotion, it was impossible this evening.

One of America's most distinguished surgeons Eugene de Savitsch was being cared for in a side room and he *was* aware of his diagnosis and its implications. I talked with him whilst looking after his bodily needs and noticed a book on his locker which, to my surprise, I had read. Even more surprising was that the author of the memoir was the patient to whom I was tending, although I hadn't realised. The book was called *In Search of Complications* which was an exciting account of Dr de Savitsch's varied and eventful life. He had been born into an aristocratic family from St Petersburg at the time of the Russian Revolution in 1917, and when he was fourteen, he had fled with his mother to Japan. Whilst other boys were still at school, Eugene was miles away sorting fish in a hotel basement or "hoisting a Russian ballerina in precarious lifts, to the astonishment of polite oriental audiences". After moving to the United States, he faced the prospect of washing dishes or starving, so he vowed to train as a doctor and became not only an eminent surgeon but also the author of *Homosexuality, Transvestism and Change of Sex*, a subject in which he was certainly ahead of his time. It was his birthday whilst I was on Fleet Street Ward and he tried hard to be cheerful as he offered Sister a celebratory taste of caviar, a present from a fellow Russian. But the sick surgeon, who looked so much older than his fifty-five years, couldn't enjoy his treat and kept calling for more and more methadone to relieve his pain saying, 'I had no idea it would be so hard to die. Why can't it be done with quickly?' As an inexperienced probationer, I felt wholly inadequate in the face of so much suffering and found the question impossible to answer.

*

Just before leaving Fleet Street Ward, I had to be weighed by the much-loved Miss Ormiston, the Sister in the Nurses' Sick Rooms, who was known universally as Ormi. I had lost weight, which wasn't surprising, and I was referred to Dr Coulson. He, dear man, "prescribed" *and* dispensed bars of chocolate as a remedy for weight loss – a very good doctor, I decided, as I shared the goodies with my friends.

There were several other pieces of news: we heard that the Queen was expecting another baby, her third, who would become the future Prince Andrew; and to celebrate the conception we treated ourselves to a cup of tea and a toasted bun at the Lyons Corner House café near Trafalgar Square. Meg joined us from St Albans and needed a bed for the night, so Priscilla, being the tallest and the bravest, daringly climbed along a window ledge of the sixth floor of the Nurses' Home to gain access to Barbara's room, which was empty because she was having a blood transfusion for her ongoing anaemia.

I had accepted, at the third time of asking, an invitation to go to the cinema with the junior houseman, which was pleasant enough until I saw that the consultant on Fleet Street Ward, Mr Robinson, was also at the viewing. He raised his eyebrows and smiled with a knowing look, and I blushed furiously.

Apart from the thought of our looming elections, where our future at the hospital was to be considered, we were a happy bunch. Election Day itself was nerve-racking; we appeared before the Board of Governors, Matron, the Sister Tutors and the Sister on whose ward we had worked. This illustrious group decided which of us had reached a high enough standard and would be privileged enough to progress with our training. Those who passed were sent through one door and those who failed through another. To my relief, I passed, despite my profligate nature with the tea and sugar, as did all my close friends, but sadly five failed – Jackie, Emma, Elizabeth, Pat and Rosemary.

Jackie's failure was no surprise. We had wondered how she had managed to get through PTS relatively unscathed considering her transgressions encompassed causing chaos with a Lambretta and dousing the place with ink. Those who did not make the grade this time had one more chance, and if they didn't make the grade the next time they would have to leave. Those of us who had been successful were now allowed to carry a basket of our own choosing and to wear a smart black and white striped Barts scarf. Apart from that, nothing had changed. We were still junior pros, and night duty beckoned.

Chapter Six

Scrambled Eggs on Toast

The list for changing wards was posted on 30th September, and I saw to my disappointment that I would be going to a women's ward called Annie Zunz. This was for a three-week orientation period before transferring to the dreaded three months of night duty.

The thought of nursing women was not appealing, and I knew I was going to miss the men's cheerful backchat and repartee. I was wrong; it *was* different, but it was equally rewarding. I found that it was possible to develop close relationships with the women, in contrast with the men where intimacy had to be avoided. Such relationships could, and did, develop but sometimes proved to be deeply upsetting in tragic cases; but, on the other hand, they also brought much pleasure.

The women tended to be more emotional than the men, but the vast majority were a pleasure to nurse. They liked to be presentable and appreciated freshly laundered sheets. A bed bath was accepted with gratitude as was the soothing application of talcum powder – Johnson's baby powder was my favourite, but I was outvoted by the patients who preferred the overpowering, sickly sweet smell of April Violets. The women's morale was boosted once their tangled hair had been gently brushed and the finishing touches of lipstick and face powder had been added. I began to understand that *care* was not all about surgery and medicine.

Many of the women on Annie Zunz were terminally ill and needed considerable support, which required mental effort and understanding on our behalf. They worried about their husbands, their children's future and their finances. Many of their problems were insurmountable, and we frequently felt unable to tackle subjects which were beyond our training but reported the troubles to Sister, who in turn notified the almoner if the worry had been financial. At eighteen, we could only be helpful listeners; we were not expected to be problem solvers, but the poverty and pain of some of the women stretched our emotions in ways we could not have anticipated.

Never a day went by without tears for one reason or another – sometimes, though, it was not the patient, but a nurse who wept, having been the recipient of Sister's lashing tongue. Indeed, I was often in trouble with Sister Annie Zunz. On one occasion, I was detailed to try and track down some missing china and was sent to several nearby wards to enquire if the offending pieces had found their way there: 'I'm sorry to bother you, Sister. I'm from Annie and I wonder if by any chance you have come across a cup, saucer and plate belonging to us?' The whereabouts of the offending china was never discovered, but I managed to receive a very firm dressing-down from Sister. Three ward Sisters, all independent of each other, reported that I had been impolite.

'I'm told you said you had come from Annie?' Sister said accusingly.

'Yes,' I replied, somewhat puzzled.

'Never, ever, let me hear you say that again. This ward is called Annie *Zunz* in memory of the Zunz family who left a generous gift in perpetuity, on condition that the ward should be named Annie *Zunz*. You were sloppy, casual and incorrect; and you must realise the importance of keeping a promise, however long ago it may have been made.'

Sister Annie Zunz was a very interesting character. She was dark-haired, young and attractive, but she was often moody and unpredictable; and even in her moods she was always very proper and precise. However, I got to see an entirely different side of her on the occasion she carried out a very intimate examination on a rather rough and elderly Eastender. She drew the curtains round the patient's bed and began the examination. Suddenly we heard loud swearing from the patient. 'Sweet Jesus! Get off me, you bastard, and bugger off!' This wasn't the end of the story. It turned out that Sister could also swear with the best. Apparently oblivious to the fact that she could be heard by the whole ward, she gave the patient as good as she got. We were astonished and rather impressed to hear her range of expletives. Her vocal retaliation worked a treat. For the rest of her stay in hospital, the old woman became sweet-tempered and docile. Surprisingly, not long after this incident, Sister Annie Zunz left the hospital to become a missionary, and I did wonder whether she ever dipped into her lexicon of foul language again.

One patient, the eighty-seven-year-old Mrs Piggott, was a favourite with us all. When asked, as was customary, to which religion she belonged, the old lady looked bemused and replied, 'Just ordinary, my dear, just ordinary.' She was endearingly innocent and typical of those bygone days when the Church of England was by far the most common denomination of the patients coming into hospital. She was always immaculate and possessed perfectly laundered fine cotton handkerchiefs smelling of lavender. Despite her frail, bird-like frame being ravaged by leukaemia, she was incredibly warm-hearted and cuddlesome. Never one to grumble, she cheerfully hoped she would die before Christmas (and her wish was granted), but in the meantime she enjoyed her many visitors. I dropped and broke four large glass fruit bowls and a cup right in front of one of them, and Mrs Piggott, ever the most polite of genteel ladies, then introduced me to her great-niece. My humiliation was complete when I found out that the visitor was none other than the Assistant Matron of the London Hospital. To give credit to Sister Annie Zunz, she saw the funny side of my mishap and did not chastise me, or rather, not until she saw the breakage board listing every item I had dropped.

*

Life was not all work, and one Saturday I went to my first-ever soccer match with Scottish Barbara to see Arsenal play Birmingham City at Highbury. I learnt that the Arsenal team were called the Gunners, apparently after the bunch of workers from the Woolwich Arsenal Factory who had laid the foundations for the club in 1886. They were kitted out in red shirts with long white sleeves, white shorts and black and white striped socks. Barbara insisted on wearing a red bobble hat and matching scarf. 'This,' she declared, 'is to show I'm supporting the home team.' We stood on one of the terraces surrounded by crowds of good-humoured men in flat caps, who were either roaring their support or groaning their disappointment. By the end I had no idea of the score or indeed who had won, but Barbara joined the ecstatic Arsenal supporters by throwing her hat in the air as she informed me that her team had won three nil.

Another day, Beth and I had a double date with two Cambridge undergraduate friends, but as she was unwell I went by myself and was treated to a hearty meal at Albert's in Beak Street and a concert conducted by Sir Thomas Beecham at the

Royal Festival Hall. I was delivered back to the hospital just as the clock was striking midnight and the main gate was closing. 'Just made it this time, Nurse,' said the night porter. 'Got two of them in tow, have you? Who's a lucky girl?'

The next day, Ormi, who could smell a potential romance a mile off, issued an invitation to the three of us to "take" tea with Beth in the Sick Rooms. All the other convalescent nurses were ordered out of the sitting room, and the four of us sat snuggly round the brightly burning fire and were served egg and cress sandwiches (their crusts cut off, of course) and delicious homemade cake, all served by Miss Ormiston on her finest bone china. We had an unexpected visitor when Miss Dye, the Home Sister, walked in on our party. 'What on earth is going on here?' she demanded. Her disapproving face was a picture, but Beth's health improved dramatically.

*

I started night duty on Annie Zunz Ward on Saturday, 14th November. It was a gruelling prospect: a forty-eight-hour week with ten consecutive nights on duty without a break. I was the first member of our set to embark on this unknown and upside-down life, which, surprisingly, gave me status, and I was presented with send-off gifts from my friends. I found a stocking outside my room filled with "electrifying" contents: an orange, a polythene bag, nuts, an empty toothpaste tube, a packet of polo mints, a packet of fruit gums and, most important of all, some "essential" iron tablets "to keep up your energy for the terrible time ahead".

At the start of my new "day", breakfast (steak and kidney pie and cabbage) was eaten, and on the dot of 7.50pm, I arrived on the ward to receive the report from Sister.

Later, when I was washing up cups and saucers in the ward kitchen, I looked out of the window and noticed a series of enthusiastic gesticulations. Black stockings were being waved, window blinds were whizzing up and down, and lights were flashing on and off. I was being greeted and treated to a display from the Nurses' Home across the way: a show of support that did much to sustain me through the coming dark hours.

As it was a weekend, we had no meal breaks away from the ward, and the first night felt very long indeed. My cleaning duties started with a vengeance after the patients had been served their nightcaps. I scrubbed, sterilised and polished what felt like hundreds of monometal bedpans until they gleamed, before giving the sluice its nightly spring clean, taking care not to wake the patients as I clanged away.

I was reminded of *The Virtues of Cleaning* as extolled by the erstwhile Matron Isla Stewart in *Murray's Magazine* in 1890:

> *Some nurses complain that they have to dust and sweep and do other household work, which could be more quickly and efficiently performed by less well-educated women. If it be true, as we are taught in these days, that absolute cleanliness is a most essential factor in the recovery of the patient then, I think, that a housemaid's work is an important part of a nurse's training and that a nurse only is efficient who can clean a room so deftly and well as not to disturb her patient. The best nurses, in realising the necessity of cleanliness, do not wish to escape from the occasional hardness implied by it.*

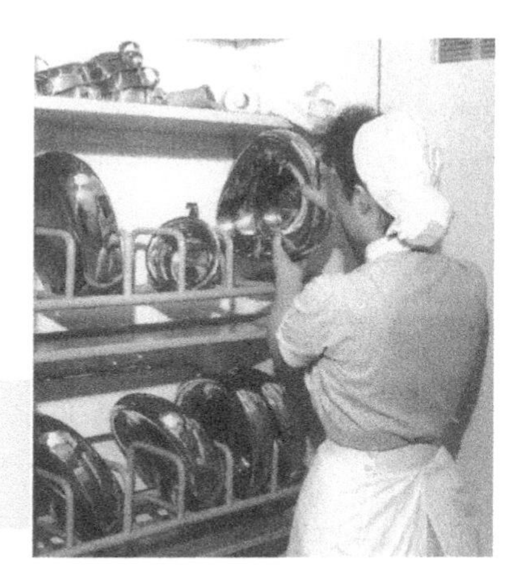

Gleaming bedpans and vomit bowls: a nightly task for the probationer nurse.

However, when it reached 1am, the virtues of cleaning were not uppermost in my mind, and my eyes felt heavy as I dreamt of being tucked up in bed. Still there was work to be done; dressings and sanitary towels (popularly called Martha pads, named after the Martha Maternity Ward) had to be rolled and packed carefully into drums in readiness for the next day's sterilisation process carried out in autoclaves. The items had to be loosely packed to allow the steam under pressure in the autoclave to penetrate all the surfaces of the articles.

Apart from taking bedpans to the needy patients and making comforting cups of tea, as well as shaking and turning pillows, rubbing backs and tidying beds, the early hours were spent virtually in the dark, standing at a table in the middle of the ward packing, packing and packing. By 3am, I thought the night would never end.

However, I had a surprise when I found out that Corinne, the third-year student nurse who was in charge of the ward, had made my tea. This was a tradition whereby the senior nurse cooked for the pro. She had made me scrambled eggs on toast, which were the best scrambled eggs I had ever tasted. 'I warn you,' she said, 'don't expect anything too gourmet. You'll get some form of egg every night as that's all there ever is in the ward kitchen.'

At 5.30am, Corinne and I started washing the very sick patients – this was strictly forbidden, but the patients were unaware of the early hour – and we managed to make every one of the twenty-seven beds – the medical wards had a larger complement of beds than the surgical wards – before the day nurses and Sister arrived on duty. Finally, the night report was given very efficiently by Corinne, and by 8.15am we were off duty at last.

I had never known such a long night and I wondered seriously how I was going to manage three months of night duty, let alone the next nine nights without a break. I was already looking forward to my four nights off.

I had to summon up enough energy to pack up all my belongings so they could be transported to the Night Nurses' Home in the West End. Task completed, I made my way wearily to St Paul's tube station and caught a train to Marble Arch before walking to the supposedly tranquil Bryanston Square. Situated some distance from the hospital, the home's peaceful situation was intended to help induce and aid sleep. Unfortunately, there was a perpetual din of banging, cement mixing and loud music blaring forth from the multiple building sites nearby. I had been forewarned and had armed myself with two new pairs of long-sleeved and long-legged floral winceyette pyjamas, a hot water bottle and bed socks, together with an eye mask to keep out the light, and ear plugs to keep out the noise. The items were bought in the vain hope of dreamless slumbers. They failed.

*

My first encounter with Lizzie Reynolds was on my second night. Lizzie was an unmarried forty-five-year-old trapeze artist from a well-known circus family. During a difficult and complex routine, she had taken a catastrophic fall and had tumbled to the ground, severing her spinal cord. In a split second, her life had changed forever. All sensation from her neck down had gone, never to return, and she became a quadriplegic doomed never to swing again from her precious trapeze and with no hope of ever walking again.

Lizzie made an immediate and intense impression upon me. She had been admitted to the hospital suffering from pneumonia, and the medical staff had already performed a tracheostomy (a surgically created hole through the front of her neck into the windpipe) to provide access to her airway so that accumulated secretions could be cleared. My first task was to learn how to suck out the secretions by using a thin catheter (flexible tube) inserted into the tracheostomy and attached to a suction machine. To my shame, I retched at the sight and smell of the foul, slimy secretions pouring forth, and poor Lizzie was sent into paroxysms of coughing each time I inserted the catheter. After I'd completed the procedure, she managed a very quiet whisper of thanks, but I was the one who was grateful for her patience and fortitude in such dire circumstances.

Over the next few months, I got to know Lizzie very well as sleep eluded her. She was unable to converse easily because of her tracheostomy, or to write messages due to her immobile hands, but her eyes remained bright and alert and her gentle smile unwavering. It was as though her life force still glowed through her increasingly translucent skin. I vowed, if I could, that I would do anything in my power to keep her alive. This vow sadly turned out to be ill judged.

There were several occasions when we thought we had lost her, and one evening at about 11.30pm Lizzie turned blue again. We managed to clear her secretions and her colour slowly returned to normal as her condition improved. We had just settled her in fresh clean sheets when to our surprise a thunderous peal of bells rang out. We had lost track of the time and were mystified for a minute until we realised that the bells from nearby St Paul's Cathedral were ringing in the New Year. All was quiet on the ward; the other patients hadn't stirred, but Lizzie smiled as I put my head close to hers and whispered, 'A Happy New Year, Lizzie.'

Ten minutes later our young Scottish houseman, Sandy Campbell, arrived on the ward a little the worse for wear. He was armed with a bottle of whisky. 'A Happy Hogmanay to both you lovely nurses. Won't you join me for a wee dram,' he said persuasively. We, of course, had to refuse; it was more than our lives were worth to be caught by the Night Sister smelling of alcohol, but we touched Lizzie's lips with the whisky and were repaid by a cheeky wink.

I noted in my journal that I would not have swapped that night for any New Year's Eve party. The comradeship, the care we had given to Lizzie and the pure clarity of sound we had experienced from the bells of St Paul's were magical and felt very grown up.

Ten days later, the doctors decided to remove Lizzie's tracheostomy tube as her neck was becoming very sore, but our fears were realised when Lizzie was unable to breathe and became unconscious. The Twilight Nurse (the Staff Nurse who worked from 4pm to midnight) started resuscitating Lizzie before medical help arrived, and as we carried on the "good" work on her silent, fragile chest, she began to recover. At last all was well. She remembered nothing. We just couldn't let her die. Not our Lizzie.

The next evening, I woke to find snow falling heavily. The journey by coach from Bryanston Square to the hospital took an age. The streets and shops looked like a scene straight from a Dickens novel. The floating snowflakes caught in the headlights of vehicles as they fell to the ground were a beautiful and unusual sight, but I couldn't stop thinking about Lizzie. Would she be alive when I went on duty? I reported to Sister and to my relief could see her in a nearby bed; she was holding her own – but only just. To her dismay, her tracheostomy tube had had to be replaced once again.

As the months passed and after I had completed my time on night duty on Annie Zunz Ward, I continued to visit Lizzie every week. Her mood had changed, and there were many times when it was clear she had suffered enough. One day, I went to pay my usual visit and found her bed occupied by another patient. My immediate fear was that she had died, but it turned out that she had been transferred to a hospital nearer to her relatives. I hadn't been able to say goodbye and could only hope that she would receive care as good as that given to her over all the months she was with us.

Six months later, in June 1961, I heard the news that Lizzie had died several months previously. My emotions were mixed. It was so sad that Lizzie had gone, but I was also relieved for her sake that she was no longer suffering. We had been told not to become too emotionally involved with our patients, and I knew that I had done just that with Lizzie. To this day, she stays with me and it is now over fifty-five years since the dreadful night when Lizzie stopped breathing. It is only recently, though, that I have discovered that the doctors who saved her life expressed regret that we had succeeded, and on reflection, they may well have been right. Certainly, if we had allowed Lizzie to die that evening she would have been spared all the extra months of dreadful suffering. It seems likely that, for the best possible motive, we had failed her.

*

My nineteenth birthday came and went; it was the first time I had spent my birthday away from home, and I felt homesick even though I received many cards and gifts. My parents sent me a special birthday cake from Fortnum & Mason, which arrived beautifully packed and was devoured by a grateful group of friends.

On the night of my birthday, I had my first experience of laying out a patient, a certain Mrs Cowley. She had begged us to allow her to die and in her last hours had kept asking us to bring her some cornflakes, which seemed so sad. Performing the last offices was daunting, but it was helped by working with Corinne, who was both empathetic and practical. I wondered whether in the future, I could be as understanding and sensitive to a junior nurse when the inevitable time came and when I would be in the position of providing reassurance.

*

During my period on night duty, I couldn't sleep during the day in spite of my preparations. Some days I only managed half an hour, and the only time I had a proper sleep during a ten-night spell was when I had a rare late call and went on duty at 11.15pm. Inevitably, on these occasions I would drift off to sleep at about 4pm just as it was getting dark, until I was rudely woken by the housekeeper at 10pm. Speech was impossible on these occasions, and my slumber continued as the coach made its way through the West End to the hospital. The Nurses' Dining Room was almost deserted, and most of the chairs were up on the tables whilst the floor was being cleaned. The pungent smell of polish mixed with the most disgusting aroma of boiled cabbage was unforgettable, and the very thought of trying to force down the "heated up" meat and two veg for my "breakfast" was repugnant.

*

There were lighter moments on night duty, and Gayle kept us amused by her exploits. On her first night on duty, she felt tired in the middle of the night, so off she popped into an empty side room for forty winks. The Night Sister had already done her round, so Gayle thought she was safe. Not a bit of it – the Night Sister had smelt a rat and came back on the ward. Gayle was in big trouble but was unrepentant.

One night, there was great excitement and fear when a murderer, known to be manic, was on the loose and had potentially been seen near the Nurses' Home. There were police everywhere, but unfortunately they were not in the ward sluice, and every time a patient wanted a bedpan I hardly dared to go into the sluice alone in case the madman jumped out at me.

On another memorable occasion, during one of our "lunch" breaks between midnight and 12.30am, six of us went for a walk, dressed in full uniform, around Smithfield Meat Market. It was a hive of activity as the meat porters rushed around heaving heavy carcasses. In spite of their activity, they still had sufficient energy and cheek to give us young women wolf whistles, which we found rather welcoming and in no way intimidating. The men made us feel as if we belonged, and for me it brought back memories of that first visit to Smithfield and the surgical display there that had so inspired me as I set off on the journey into the unknown.

Another foray in the dark was on the night of 31st January, at 11.48pm. After a quick "lunch" we decided to go to St Paul's Cathedral to "hear in" the new month. Six of us, again in full uniform, ran for all our worth, disregarding the hospital rule that running was only allowed in cases of fire and haemorrhage. We arrived as the clock began to strike twelve and collapsed in laughter on the grand steps of the famous cathedral. The City of London was very quiet but its very tranquility seemed to welcome us as we sat absorbing the atmosphere of centuries gone by.

During our period of night duty, Beth and I spent one of our spells of four nights off in Cambridge, where there *was* romance in the air. We fancied undergraduates both of whom were called John. On arrival in this seat of academia, I was taken aback – I had never, ever, seen so many men. They were *everywhere*. University life, compared to our cloistered existence, seemed very disorganised and casual; students appeared to roll up to lectures as and when they felt like it. The boys hired bikes for us and we all cycled energetically around Cambridge enjoying the magnificent colleges, the clear blue sky and the golden daffodils, which were heralding spring. We stayed at an excellent bed and breakfast and cooked lunch for eight or so students – our tutoring in scrambled egg-making at PTS was proving worthwhile. The thought of going back to night duty was not so appealing; we had to be back at Bryanston Square by 2.30pm, when the doors were locked behind us. Coming down from the euphoric freedom of our blissful break, we were far too restless to be able to sleep, so we played Charles Trenet singing *La Mer* on Beth's tape recorder continuously until we went on duty.

Ten days later, my time on Annie Zunz came to an end. I had been on duty since 7.50pm the previous evening and it was 9.50am by the time Sister had finished going through my practical procedures chart. She was unexpectedly complimentary, and although I shouldn't have wanted praise, it gave me such a glow of contentment that I felt that perhaps the hours of cleaning, making comforting cups of tea and giving out bedpans were worth it after all. I was sad to say goodbye to the patients, many of whom, in their own way, had taught me so much.

The number in our set was dwindling fast. We were down to thirty – Emma, Elizabeth and Rosemary and, unsurprisingly, "could-I-catch-it" Jackie had failed their elections again. So, that was that. The poor girls who had set out with such high expectations were immediately dismissed. Meanwhile, the rest of us were off on a fortnight's holiday, and a group of us were going for a week to the ski slopes, which cost us £28 of our very hard-earned money. I had already spent £8 19s 6d on a very expensive pair of ski trousers from Swan and Edgars at Piccadilly Circus, but I kept it to myself.

Chapter Seven

Bags, Bottoms and the Steam Tent

Sister Abernethy was working at her desk, surrounded by scattered papers and temperature charts. Her reputation went before her; she did indeed look as mad as a hatter and totally disorganised. I stood there for a while before she noticed me.

'Hello, dear. What can I do for you?' She lifted her head, revealing her "salt and pepper" hair escaping from her Sister's cap, and gave me a somewhat preoccupied and worried glance.

'I'm reporting for duty, Sister.'

'Oh, are you? That's excellent. We could do with another pair of hands. Could you just pop to the greengrocer to buy some mushrooms?'

Mushrooms? It was my turn to look bemused. What on earth had mushrooms got to do with running a women's surgical ward?

'I'm planning to cook chips, eggs and mushrooms to try and tempt a patient to eat, and I don't have any mushrooms and it was mushrooms Mrs Davies really fancied.'

So, *this* was why everyone enjoyed working on Abernethy – the patient came first. I was not surprised that Sister was loved by patients and nurses alike.

During my three months on Abernethy Ward, I never did find out whether Sister's apparent absent-mindedness and anxious appearance were genuine or just pretence as she viewed us all with a twinkle in her eye. It was clear that she had a heart of gold, and the understanding care she gave to her patients was without question. She was a worker, and there was nothing she expected her nurses to do that she wouldn't roll up her sleeves for and do herself. We learnt by her example.

Sister Abernethy followed in the footsteps of the diminutive Kathleen Raven, who, some years back, had been a Sister on the same ward and was always affectionately known as the Pocket Battleship – a reference to her lack of inches and to her fearlessness in pursuing high standards of patient care. It was said that Kathleen Raven and our statuesque Matron (Joan Loveridge) had attended their training interview on the same day. Joan was heard to say, 'If they require them short, you will be in; if they require them tall, I'll be all right.' As it turned out for the benefit of the nursing profession, they were both "all right".

During the war years, Kathleen lived in a room off Abernethy Ward and for two years cheerfully slept on an air mattress. She was a brave woman, and during the night when the hospital was hit, and 7,000 Londoners were killed and a further 9,000 injured, she was blown across Casualty but said that it had never entered her head that she might herself have been killed. She went on to have a very distinguished career and became Matron at the Leeds Infirmary, where she opened two "beau parlours", described as "comfortable little rooms where a nurse may entertain her men friends" – what an enlightened woman! After Leeds, she moved to the Ministry of Health and rose to become the country's Chief

Nursing Officer and was subsequently appointed a Dame of the British Empire. Later in life, she lamented the end of on-the-ward apprenticeships in 1988 and expressed her concern over the greater emphasis on academic training for nurses. She feared that computers rather than patients were increasingly the focus of attention, and that clipboards and not the sick were being clasped to the bosom.

Apart from general surgery, the "firm", led by two senior consultants, specialised in rectal surgery and urinary tract abnormalities. I learnt much from Sister Abernethy about bottoms, bladders and stoma care as we all worked together under the watchful eyes of the two very eminent gentlemen.

Mr Clifford Naunton Morgan (later to become Sir Clifford) was the famous little Welshman who used to arrive in the Square in his super-large Bentley with his head barely visible above the steering wheel. He was the first to perform the life-saving operation for patients who had rectal cancer. This radical, as well as very personal, operation involved the removal of the patient's anus, rectum and part of the intestine and the diversion of a section of the large intestine through an opening in the abdomen where the body waste was collected in a bag. Fortunately, the surgeon, known for his boundless energy, kindness and lack of pomposity, had an ability to make his patients laugh. His puckish sense of humour and advice frequently referred to the nether regions of the body. He would stand at the end of the patient's bed and would turn to one of his dressers (medical student) and interrogate them: 'Have you listened for bowel sounds?'

'Yes, sir.'

'Did you hear any?'

'Yes, sir.'

'Excellent. Has the patient passed flatus?'

'Yes, sir.'

Turning to the patient and to his dressers, the great man declared, 'Where there is wind, there is a way; and what you have to know is that what sounds obnoxious to a duchess, sounds like music in a surgeon's ear.'

Mr Naunton Morgan was also sympathetic towards his nurses. One morning, when he was conducting his ward round, I cut my finger and broke a full coffee pot, spilling the entire contents of scalding liquid at his feet. I blushed and my shame was complete when I became aware of the sniggers and smirking faces of his entourage of students. However, from the chief himself there were no recriminations, just a jovial 'Bad luck, Nurse.'

The other player in the partnership, Mr Dennis Ellison Nash, was of a much more serious nature, although he too wasn't without a sense of humour. We heard of the time, during an operation, when a student inadvertently kept his foot on the diathermy pedal when the diathermy point came into contact with a wet patch on the front of Mr Nash's gown. The surgeon experienced an intense pain in his chest and was convinced he had had a heart attack and stepped back from the operating table to make peace with his maker. To his astonishment and delight, the pain immediately disappeared. When he found out the cause of his "heart attack", it made him rather suspicious, but apparently he was so pleased still to be alive that he told nobody.

Mr Nash was a devout Christian, who appeared somewhat forbidding due, apparently, to his shyness. He, like his colleague, was a surgical pioneer and was the first surgeon in Britain to carry out the intricate operation of grafting the ureters (the tubes that carry urine from the kidneys to the bladder) onto the intestine, which served the purpose as a replacement bladder. A spout (a small protrusion of the intestine) was then brought onto the surface of the abdomen, and a bag was fixed over the spout in which to collect the urine.

Both types of the complicated surgery carried out by the two surgeons were finalised with a crudely formed bag in which to collect bodily fluids. I was still a probationer, and as far as I was concerned, the intake and output of the patient was of the utmost importance. Why else did pros spend so much time in the kitchen and the sluice? On the ward, there were colostomy bags in which to collect faecal matter and urostomy bags for urine in abundance. Both sorts were continually waiting to be applied and to be emptied; this was a challenge for both patients and junior nurses alike. Disposable gloves were an item of the future and where it was deemed necessary – which was rare – to wear gloves, these were made of rubber and after use were washed, powdered and re-sterilised. Tow, which was made of hemp fibre, was invaluable for "mopping up" purposes.

In late March, a lively, wheelchair-bound, sixteen-year-old girl called Anne, from Aldershot, arrived on the ward accompanied by her parents and her younger brother Billy. Unlike her deeply worried mother and father, the teenager was excited and carefree.

Anne was paralysed from the waist down due to a condition called spina bifida, where her spine and spinal cord had not developed properly when she was in the womb, and this had caused a gap in her spine. Born before the days of the ultra-scan, it was not until her birth that Anne's condition could be seen and was diagnosed. The news was devastating for her parents, and the inescapable outcome for Anne was lifelong incontinence. Now approaching adulthood, she was still wearing embarrassingly voluminous bloomers and white terry towelling nappies. Mr Nash's revolutionary operation was her chance to get rid of the soggy, smelly nappies forever – she could hardly wait.

On 2nd May 1960, she gallantly underwent the unpleasant pre-operative enemas, washouts and pill preparations. Then came the best bit. 'Right, Anne,' I joked. 'Let's have those big baggy bloomers off.' We rejoiced together as I removed her knickers and her nappy for what we both thought would be the last time. The jubilation was short-lived. At the very last minute, Mr Nash decided to postpone the surgery; he had carried out this new operation on another of our patients a few days earlier, and complications had suddenly, and dramatically, arisen and he was very concerned.

A week later, all the preparation started again. This time, when I removed Anne's nappies, our mood was muted. The operation finally went ahead and Anne even managed a weak, sleepy smile when she woke several hours later.

The next few days were crucial, and it was a very anxious time for her parents, both wondering whether they should have agreed to put their daughter through such a major and unproven operation. The curtains remained pulled round Anne's bed and she was surrounded by apparatus and equipment whilst she was given blood transfusions and other intravenous fluids and the senior nursing staff attended to her dressings. We all willed her to get better.

A week after her operation, she was out of the critical stage, and her eyes began to sparkle at the thought of her "dry" life ahead. Her spout was ceremoniously named Elly after Mr Ellison Nash, and after two weeks she tried to take a few faltering steps. The brave girl would not give up, but I realised that in spite of the major operation she had undergone, she would still remain wheelchair-bound for the rest of her life.

I remained friends with Anne after she eventually left the hospital, and, when the time came, she attended my wedding. She herself married in 1970 but telephoned me one day to say she was going to be a nun. This was a surprise indeed. In fact, it turned out that I had misheard and that what she had said was she was going to be a mum, and she became the proud mother of Mark. Over the years, Anne has had breast cancer and sadly lost her husband, Peter, also from cancer, but she remains as courageous and determined as ever and lives a very happy, independent life.

It's almost sixty years since she underwent Mr Ellison Nash's groundbreaking operation. She tells me with gratitude that "Elly" has never faltered and is still referred to by that illustrious name.

*

As we all moved slowly up the ladder of the pro hierarchy we were never allowed to forget that the *care* of the patient was our prime objective which, of course, went hand in hand with skill and knowledge in carrying out a variety of procedures. This was in the days when Health and Safety at Work regulations were a twinkle in a bureaucrat's eye and we had little protection from workplace injuries. One day, whilst I was working on Abernethy, I gave a routine pre-operative injection to a patient and managed to break the glass ampoule, the contents of which sprayed into one of my eyes and gave me a very alluring dilated pupil. The "allure" left me after a couple of hours when the pupil went back to its pinprick self, and it didn't even occur to me to report the incident to Sister.

It was around this time that I was permitted to care for the unconscious patients recovering from minor surgery procedures as they returned from the operating theatre. There were no recovery rooms alongside the operating theatre, and the patients came back from their surgery deeply asleep, which was quite worrying, and they had to be watched with care. An artificial airway was in place, and when the patient woke, they tended to spit it out and then vomit.

Our first anniversary at the hospital arrived on Wednesday 4th May. I had never known a year go by so quickly, and I noted

The attainment of a striped belt denoted the rise to a second-year nurse.

in my journal that I had absolutely no regrets. The "striping" list went up on the notice board, and those of us who were successful had our plain grey belts replaced by striped ones made of the same material as our uniform dress. This change in our uniform may have been small, but it signified that we had reached the exalted position of a second-year nurse. No longer a pro but a second-year nurse! I strutted proudly around the ward until I realised it had made no difference to my day – there were no pros on the ward, and I was still the most junior and therefore was back at the bedpans and responsible for removing flowers on the patients' lockers before the night staff came on duty.

Not everybody was happy, though. Poor Meg, now back with us in London, was very run-down and found it hard to sleep and so was sent home for a few days to recuperate. Two others said they were planning to leave, and a third, an academic girl called Ruth who had gained top marks in our PTS examinations and whose father was a headmaster, said she already had a job lined up as a telephonist at £6 4s 0d (£6.20) a week, whereas our pay was still under £3 a week; but on the other hand, we did live in, all our meals were paid for, and we were housed in a prime location in the Square Mile of the City of London.

The wearing of uniform was obligatory even in the classroom.

I left Abernethy for a month to attend Study Block in preparation for our preliminary state examinations. It didn't take me long to decide that I preferred working and learning by example from those senior to me on the ward to being taught in the classroom, but the good news was that in Block the hours were from 8.30am until 4.30pm, and we had Saturday afternoons and Sundays off. This very welcome change in our routine made us feel human again and allowed us to take part in various activities.

There were times when I pined for the country, and during my spell on Block I managed to get home for the occasional weekend where I could enjoy the peace and quiet compared with the chaos of London. I was totally spoiled by my parents on my return visits. They were always eager to hear my news and never tired of welcoming my friends who often turned up with me at short notice. We were always treated to my favourite meal – roast chicken with all the trimmings followed by homemade raspberry trifle. My mother's roast potatoes were second to none.

One day, Priscilla and I went to watch the Oxford and Cambridge Boat Race on the Thames and enjoyed seeing the dark blues of Oxford trounce the light blues of Cambridge; this was much better than having to watch a grainy recording of their triumph on a black and white television. At Mortlake, I caught an unseen glimpse of Walter, the schoolmaster who had had the audacity to telephone me at PTS. He was on the riverbank with his arm around the shoulders of a very attractive-looking girl; I couldn't help but feel just a twinge of envy.

On Sunday 22nd May, several of us went to watch the Ceremony of the Keys at the Tower of London where the Chief Beefeater, dressed in his traditional red and carrying a candle in one hand and the Queen's keys in the other, performed the gate-closing ritual with three of his fellow Beefeaters. In all its 700-year history, this nightly event had never been cancelled and was delayed only once during the Second World War when a bomb knocked a couple of Beefeaters off their feet. There was a real sense of history during the short ceremony which was made all the more atmospheric by the floodlit castle. It ended as the Chief Beefeater raised his Tudor bonnet high in the air and called, 'God preserve Queen Elizabeth.' The guard answered 'Amen' as the clock chimed 10pm and the Duty Drummer sounded *The Last Post* on his bugle, and we were escorted to the exit without delay at exactly 10.05pm.

During our time in Study Block we were woken at about 1am one night by incessant bell ringing, which was getting nearer and nearer to the Nurses' Home. I leapt out of bed and pulled my threadbare chintz curtains to one side and looked out of my window. Two fire engines were approaching at high speed, and two policemen on foot were racing up the road towards the hospital. Was the hospital on fire? I joined Meg and Priscilla on the corridor of the sixth floor where there was already a mêlée of chattering nurses, when a unanimous decision was made to climb up onto the roof of the Nurses' Home. This, we felt, would be the safest and most practical place from which to be rescued. I must admit, the vision of a dramatic act by a handsome fireman on his extended ladder, encompassing us in his tender arms, was not far from our thoughts. This romantic notion, however, did not come to pass; the hospital was not being burnt to the ground, and it turned out the flames were pouring out of the nearby window of the building opposite.

The bevy of Sisters who had joined us on the roof were neither shocked nor dishevelled, but they no longer had the look of authority to which we were accustomed. They were an amazing sight, and, for us, the most interesting aspect of the entire fire episode was the chance to view their different forms of night attire. To our disappointment, not one was wearing a revealing negligée or was adorned in fashionable satin. Most were wearing long cotton nightdresses which could be viewed trailing over their fluffy slippers, accessorised by an assortment of multi-coloured candlewick dressing gowns. Sister Butlin arrived on the scene with her hair rolled in separate pin curls, each secured by a hairpin and all kept in place by a big brown hairnet. We could hardly control our mirth.

This wasn't our only free entertainment. Tickets for theatre performances in London were given to the hospital specifically for the nurses. Sometimes six of us would squeeze into a taxi so we could get back to the Nurses' Home by the 10.30pm curfew. On countless occasions, we were given a free or a greatly reduced fare by the kind cockney taxi drivers. 'This,' they always said, 'is to thank you nurses for what you do for us.'

*

Late June arrived, and it was the season for the Oxford and Cambridge White Tie Balls. In the 1960s, there was a dearth of women studying at the two elite universities, and it wasn't until 1979 that the fairer sex were universally accepted to take a place on equal footing with the men. Nurses from the London Teaching Hospitals reaped the benefit of this shortage, and many of us received sought-after invitations. Jane, our "head girl", was one of the lucky ones as was Beth who was due to go off to Cambridge for her May Ball, and I was also planning my wardrobe for *my* Commemoration Ball in Oxford.

However, before these much-anticipated events took place, there was, as far as Beth was concerned, a personal, and in her eyes, a major calamity. In preparation for the ball, she had borrowed an evening dress from her aunt, and unbeknown to me she had nominated Priscilla as her coiffeur extraordinaire. The "appointment" had gone well and without incident. Later, I saw Beth wearing a headscarf which completely covered her hair, and I assumed she had seen a professional hairdresser.

'A good trip to the hairdresser's?' I asked.

She scowled. 'Just don't ask me about my hair.'

'A good trip to the hairdresser's?' I repeated more firmly this time.

'I didn't go to the hairdresser's.'

She removed the headscarf furtively to reveal that she no longer had fair hair, but it was now brilliant and brassy, not even red, but an "orange phenomenon".

'Beth! What *have* you done?'

'I just thought it would be a good idea to have a few copper highlights and look what's happened. It's called Golden Leopard,' she wailed.

We had to find a solution. This was just two days before the long-awaited ball, and we mounted a "Save Beth's Hair Fund" to raise the inordinately expensive £9 which was required to dye her locks back to their original state. She did, however, have to go on duty that evening. It was as well her cap covered up 75% of the result of her ill-fated amateur hairdressing session.

I was already looking forward to *my* ball at Oxford and had decided what to wear. My white, three-quarter length, broderie anglaise off-the-shoulder dress had a modest prettily scooped neckline and would, I felt, be perfect for such an event. Worn with deep blue satin gloves and matching shoes, I was confident the ensemble would fit the bill admirably.

I arrived late in Oxford on the day of the ball due to my afternoon duties, and I barely had time to change into my finery. However, after a quick brush of my hair and a careful application of Yardley's soft red "Lip Slicker" (which the advert assured me would add a hint of sheen to my lips) and a dab of "Blue Grass" eau de parfum behind each ear, I felt pretty stylish.

It was a balmy evening, and the ancient Trinity College in Broad Street was impressive with its extensive lawn and expansive gardens in which we sipped our early evening cocktails.

Most of the young ladies were dressed in long, very elegant, low cut or strapless evening dresses. They had fashionable bouffant or beehive hairstyles, and their faces were skillfully made-up. I presumed hours had been spent smoothing on their cream make-up, grooming, shaping and defining their eyebrows, applying eyeshadow and mascara before finally painting their lips in bright lipstick and adding a triumphant dab of face powder. They looked lovely and so sophisticated.

My pure white dress no longer seemed appropriate. It was not long, and it certainly wasn't strapless or low cut; my hair was flat due to the previous hours of wearing a cap and my soft red "Lip Slicker" was barely noticeable and hardly the height of fashion.

There were a few brave avant-garde girls who had not followed tradition and were wearing very short skirts, had spiky haircuts and wore no make-up whatsoever. It didn't seem to matter to which of the two groups one belonged, the stylish or the trendy, but I didn't seem to fit into either.

After a delicious dinner which was held in college, we danced the night away in one of two huge marquees. There were two apparently well-known bands, although I hadn't heard of either, and I was taught a dance which was new to me called rock 'n' roll. This was danced with tremendous energy to an amazing piece called *Rock Around the Clock* by Bill Haley and the Comets – I loved it.

A beautiful dawn broke at 4am, and to my relief we went punting on the river. My escort, Ian, was an expert with the pole, and this was a perfect excuse for me to have a sleep without the fear of recrimination from a Night Sister. We had breakfast at an all-night café in Oxford which was full of debauched, obviously hungover undergraduates who looked much the worse for wear, and I had a thumping headache, which wasn't surprising.

Attending the ball was a pleasurable occasion, but it felt quite shallow and a world away from nursing patients. I wasn't sure whether I would ever like to repeat the experience. My train left Oxford for London at 6am and by 7.30am I was back on Abernethy Ward to work another full day. Meanwhile, "Head Girl" Jane didn't arrive back on her ward after her ball until 8.30am, and to her and everyone else's surprise, the Ward Sister hadn't even noticed she was missing.

Now, firmly back in our real world, the Preliminary Practical Examination loomed ever nearer. Again, I was exempt from the theory as I had passed Human Biology at 'O' level when I was at school and so was the envy of many in our set. Nevertheless, the practical had to be taken and passed. During a recent practical class, one of our tutors, Miss Bailey, had told me she would have failed me three times over, which was hardly encouraging. I wasn't the only one who was admonished. The tutor was a stickler for correctness and lost no time in dealing out her pessimistic predictions; it was possibly a ploy to keep us on our toes. Praise and encouragement was not her way of engendering a high standard of nursing care.

The exam was held at Moorfield's Eye Hospital, and I remember the designated room of doom as if it was yesterday. It was antiquated and divided into examination cubicles by the positioning of screens behind which were various "volunteer" patients (out-of-work actors) with a wide variety of diagnoses and problems. Some of the patients required a simple procedure such as the application of a bandage or a straightforward dressing, which didn't cause me a problem. However, this was not the case for the *very sick* gentleman in the final cubicle. In his case, two of us examinees had to join forces and make a steam tent.

We were both aghast. 'Can you remember how to make a steam tent?' I whispered.

'No idea,' she replied.

Apart from the pathetic effort we had made on our lovely Victoria at PTS, neither of us had given steam tents any further thought.

'Well, we know the patient has to be in bed, so that's a start,' I volunteered. 'And then we can try and construct a tent over him.'

We racked our brains to try and remember what was required but to no avail.

My bright partner made an intelligent suggestion: 'How about a large sheet and a screen to provide the canopy?'

Good thinking. At last some progress was being made.

'I think that somewhere in the back of my mind we were told we needed a kettle of boiling water, a wall thermometer and safety pins,' I offered.

We had learnt the theory and were beginning to remember what items were required, but we were then faced with the practical application of making the tent. We discovered that neither of us had been a Girl Guide. I had been a leprechaun in the Brownie pack, but this wasn't really much use. The patient smiled encouragingly as we made our feeble attempt. We put the screen around the head of the bed, which formed three sides of a rectangle, and then put the white sheet over the top of the screen and tried to secure it neatly with the safety pins. We knew the final result should have been neat and symmetrical; ours was not. However, we were quite pleased with our handiwork and turned away from the patient to assemble the other items required to go under the tent.

'Nurses, Nurses. Quick,' the patient whispered urgently.

The tent was no more; it had sagged and then fallen dramatically over the head of the patient. I peeped under the sheet and saw the man shaking with laughter with his finger in his mouth, hollering (quietly) as if he was a Red Indian.

To my great surprise, and probably that of Miss Bailey, I managed to pass the Preliminary Practical Examination (as did my partner in crime); although how, I shall never know.

Chapter Eight

Scrubbing Up

It was not yet 7.30am, but Miss Bartlett was already in her party frock – a very plain, almost floor-length, sleeveless, green fine denim dress with two large pockets on each side of the skirt. She was wearing a pair of plimsoll-type shoes, and on her head was a green turban, which completely covered her hair. "Belinda", as she was universally known, was the Superintendent of Theatres. She was a statuesque middle-aged woman with piercingly blue eyes and had a reputation for not suffering fools gladly. Barely had she said good morning to me in her clipped tones before she launched into her obviously well-rehearsed homily.

'Today, Nurse Tisdale, whilst the operations are in progress, you will keep out of the way and not *touch* anything. However, you must *watch* everything very carefully indeed. You will notice a well-oiled routine and swift but controlled activity. Many hours of preparation by my team have already taken place today in readiness for the surgeon. Over the next few months, *you* will be carrying some of the responsibility for the successful preparation and outcome of many operations. It goes without saying that you must be hard-working and conscientious and adhere to specific routines and understand the reasons why we undertake them. You need to be able to think quickly and have the confidence to act instantly, often in circumstances of great emotional tension and technical complexity. Do you understand?'

Barely giving herself time to draw a breath, she continued: 'You will find that the operating theatre bears little resemblance to ward work and the care of the patients. Your contact with the patient will be brief and sometimes not at all.'

My heart sank.

'It is vital that you understand the importance of coordinated teamwork and that you are able to work happily and loyally as part of the team. This, of course, is ultimately for the benefit of the patient. Finally, I would like to draw to your attention the importance of cleanliness as you will find that cleaning will be a large part of your duties, particularly as I am aware you are coming here on night duty.'

Once Belinda's lecture had come to a close, she strode off, telling me she needed to "scrub up", whatever that meant.

I took off my uniform and put on a party frock. Nobody seemed to know why this decidedly non-couture item of clothing was so named. It had the look of a prison garment, which was probably why, in hospital jargon, it was called a "party frock". I slipped a pair of ill-fitting plimsolls on my feet before being faced with a square of fine green cotton material. Not *another* millinery masterpiece? Fortunately, whilst pleating was required, unlike the fiasco at PTS, this time there were no pretty white tails to fashion, and I was able to create a fairly reasonable turban that completely covered my hair. I put on a face mask to cover my nose and mouth and was told it should never be touched by my fingers. This whole rigmarole, unsurprisingly, was called "getting dressed in greens", purely and simply because everything was green, including me as a first-timer.

The boilers were bubbling ferociously – there was no central sterilisation in 1960, and everything had to be boiled for two minutes by a kitchen timer. The atmosphere was steamy, and sweaty nurses were dishing up numerous metal bowls and instruments with forceps called Cheatles. They appeared to know exactly what they were doing as I heard them mumble unrecognisable names such as tobies and stills, Bozeman needle holder, Kocher's intestinal clamp and a Periosteal elevator. A junior nurse rushed into the sterilising room carrying a large metal bowl and a pair of forceps.

'What's a Dossett and where will I find it?'

There was general mirth when she was informed Dossett was not a surgical instrument but Henry Dossett, the theatre orderly. She was embarrassed and had my sympathy. I, too, would have made the same mistake. I obviously had a lot to learn – fast. Henry and Jock – the other orderly, who could always be found in the theatre lobby smoking a cigarette under the No Smoking sign – were very experienced, and both proved to be invaluable allies and generous with their considerable knowledge and expertise.

By now, there was activity in the scrub and gowning area of the operating theatre, and I could see this routine was laborious. The surgeon and his assisting Theatre Sister, Miss Corfield, scrubbed their hands and forearms for a full five minutes before they were helped into their sterile gowns.

Next came, what seemed to me, a very complicated exercise. The gowned couple dusted their hands with powder before they "gloved up". The left glove was picked up by its fold with the right hand and drawn on. The right glove was then picked up by inserting the gloved fingers of the left hand inside the fold. The left thumb held the cuff of the right sleeve in place whilst the fingers turned the fold of the glove over it. The left glove was then drawn down. Et Voila!

Whatever next? Would I *ever* remember this procedure?

*

On that first day, I remained in the background and watched with fascination as the operations were being carried out. There was normal everyday conversation taking place over the patients' unconscious bodies; this was not what I had envisaged or expected. The exchanges were not without humour, and the consultant couldn't resist reporting a little gem from his early morning round that day, when he had addressed a dear old soul who was sitting up in bed sipping her cup of tea.

'I said to her, "Have you been bedridden much?" To which she replied without hesitation, "Yes, sir, thousands of times and twice in a rowing boat."'

We all enjoyed the surgeon's tale, and the oblivious patient on the operating table was blissfully unaware of our laughter.

The best bit of the long day came at 4pm. Trays of sandwiches with their crusts cut off arrived for all the theatre staff – surgeons and nurses alike. These were made by the very popular Shirley from the theatre workroom. There was a variety of different fillings in the delicately prepared sandwiches, including egg and cress, tinned salmon with thinly sliced cucumber and sandwich spread. This daily tradition was much anticipated and appreciated by everyone. There was no hierarchical structure during the break, and the surgeons had to wash up their own mugs after the tea party before getting back to work.

After the completion of the operating list, the surgical team disrobed and departed, leaving us to clean up and clear up.

Suddenly the atmosphere changed and could have been cut with a knife. A TOWEL CLIP WAS MISSING! All hell was let loose.

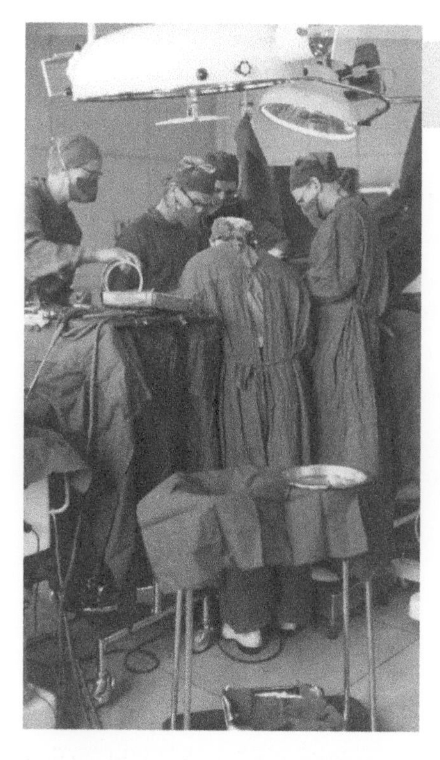

The surgeons and Theatre Sister intent on their work.

I was told to check every piece of dirty and bloody linen that had been used throughout the day. Others were detailed to count and recount the instruments, the used swabs and the dirty dressings. The clip was nowhere to be seen. An awful thought began to dawn: could it have found its way into the abdomen of one of the patients? We continued our search for a further ninety minutes.

'It's here!' The bringer of good news had found the offending clip in an instrument tray, hidden within one that was exactly the same. Relief – at least the clip wasn't residing within a patient; what wasn't so good was that we were all an hour and a half late going off duty.

*

A week later and everything was beginning to click into place, and I was starting to learn the names of the various forceps, needle holders, clamps, etc. I admired Miss Corfield not only for her skill but for the manner in which she controlled the workings of her theatre and her firm and friendly demeanour.

It was a privilege to watch the surgeons operate and to listen to the good-humoured banter, although on more than one occasion the gorgeous surgeon Mr Todd could be heard yelling angrily at the houseman, 'That fluid should be going into the patient's rectum, not into my boots, you idiot.'

Dr George Elliot, the anaesthetist, was a sight to behold as he sat in the operating theatre at the head of his unconscious patients with his cane cigarette holder clamped between his teeth. His colleague Dr Alan Lodge always put his lighted cigarette on the windowsill whilst he intubated (put a tube into the patient's windpipe) and then resumed smoking as soon as the patient was safely under.

On the whole, the consultants treated us nurses well. I had expected to come across one or two Sir Lancelot Spratts (the infamous surgeon written about in the *Dr in the House* book by ex-Barts man Richard Gordon alias Gordon Ostlere, which I had read countless times). The fictitious Sir Lancelot Spratt was the operating theatre god who had a white linen suit freshly starched and carefully warmed by a junior nurse every day before commencing his operating list. The arrogant man expected the Sister to know which instrument he required; and if she made a mistake, he calmly dropped the wrong instrument on the floor and was known to tip a whole trayful of instruments ceremoniously in an unsterile heap at his feet.

No wonder I was apprehensive about real-life situations.

Although some of the younger "gods" seemed to enjoy their elevated status and could be overbearing, the majority were perfect gentlemen. Sir James Paterson Ross, in particular, was known for his impeccable manners and was renowned for holding doors open for even the most junior of student nurses.

Belinda, though, was a hard taskmaster and was always spying on us. She was in overall charge of all the operating theatres and had a habit of entering any one of them unannounced, ready to pounce on an unsuspecting student. Unfortunately, I was often the recipient of her wrath.

'Nurse Tisdale, what *do* you think you are doing? I saw you touch the lamp and you now have "dirty hands". She frogmarched me to the scrubbing area and watched as I shamefacedly washed the invisible dirt away. All the while she berated me. 'Have you never heard of Joseph Lister who was Professor of Surgery at Glasgow University in the late 1800s? It was he who found that cleanliness was vital in the operating theatre and that germs carried on the fingers were an important cause of infection.'

In Belinda's view, cleanliness was indeed next to godliness. Three weeks later, I was on night duty and then the cleaning would really start.

*

The long hours of hospital life were starting to get some people down. Two more of our set, Pat and Helen, departed for a more normal life; Meg and Priscilla went home to discuss with their parents whether they could manage to carry on; but both, thankfully, were encouraged to remain; and Carol, one of the PTS Lambretta girls, gave in her notice as she was leaving to marry a delicious young medical student called Rupert.

To make matters worse, one day, my long-standing ally Beth seemingly disappeared off the face of the earth. I spent many hours searching for her until eventually I learned that she had been admitted to Annie Zunz Ward having been diagnosed with tuberculosis. The poor girl had had four tomographs (detailed X-rays) that morning, which had shown "shadows" on both her lungs and had been told she would not be working for at least six months.

My thoughts ran away with me, and I half expected to find a pale, feverish patient delicately coughing up blood and lying pathetically against her pillows à la Beth March in *Little Women*. But no, she was sitting up in bed with a big grin on her face.

'You know what this means, don't you?' she said bravely. 'Three months at home in the country with my mother's wholesome cooking and then three months convalescing on the ski slopes in Davos with the compliments of St Bartholomew's Hospital.'

It would seem that little had changed on the TB front since a village doctor, who had studied at Barts, had pioneered a radical treatment for his tuberculosis patients. In 1840, Dr George Boddington wrote an essay noting that *most* important in the cure of consumption was fresh air and early morning walks as well as a nutritious diet and "a proper quantity" of wine. The essay was violently attacked by the medical journal *The Lancet* and was condemned by those in higher authority, but when Boddington died in 1882, his obituary in *The Lancet* acknowledged that the doctor had anticipated by many years the modern approach to the treatment of the disease. Indeed, Beth's "prescription" in 1961 was based largely on the advice given by this village doctor nearly a hundred years earlier, and she admitted to looking forward to "the proper quantity" of wine being administered.

'Farewell, my friend,' she said. 'I'll be back. Don't worry.'

Meg and I packed up all Beth's belongings, feeling rather bereft. Despite her reassurances, it felt so final.

*

The Duty Theatre was lit throughout the night and kept us alert and ready for emergencies. I was one of two junior nurses, and there was a "Pink" in charge until midnight, after which she left us to carry out specific duties whilst she remained on call.

One of the junior's tasks was to "wall wash". This task was carried out using very, very long-handled mops dipped in carbolic solution with which every inch of *all* six operating theatre walls had to be washed thoroughly. The chore was backbreaking, cricked-neck inducing and exhausting. On completion of each wall wash, sterile utensils for use the next day had to be dished up and placed on towelled stainless steel tables – this was known as "laying up the side". Before doing this, I had to gown up and put on sterile gloves at *each* port of call.

The dark, deserted operating theatres were scary enough, but they were nothing compared to the back stairs of the theatre block. These stairways were poorly lit and decidedly spooky. I had heard that some nurses carried the Savage decompressor, a lethal instrument, as a form of protection against possible intruders. My method was to sprint up the flights of stairs as fast as I could. One evening, at about midnight, as I was going up, I suddenly heard footsteps approaching. I braced myself for fight or flight and ended up going headlong into none other than the ubiquitous Belinda dressed in full theatre regalia. She was obviously still working.

'Calm down, Nurse Tisdale. Calm down. I'm not a ghost, you know. I see you are not injured, that's a relief. Have a good night and keep up the good work.'

I would have forgiven her even if she had broken my leg – this was praise indeed, and her encouraging words spurred me on to continue, with renewed vigour, the boring three-hour round of wall washing, laying up, gowning up and gloving up. In fact, that night I almost enjoyed myself.

Inevitably, there were some nights when we were very busy, but there were quiet periods during which we welcomed the chance to learn. We had a lesson on how to "take" an appendectomy from our Pink, Helen Jolly. We laid up the instrument trolley, wheeled it to the operating table and towelled up the invisible patient. We were ready to start when Sandy Campbell, the erstwhile Hogmanay house physician from Annie Zunz Ward, arrived. Our beautiful Helen blushed, and I wondered whether they had perhaps taken a shine to each other.

There was no time for romance, though. There was work to do, and he was asked if he would like to pose as the patient. He declined in horror but reappeared and tenderly laid a jelly baby on the operating table as a replacement. The powerful operating light was turned on and we were ready to go. Sad to say that even before a knife had been lifted, the jelly baby met its early demise and melted before our very eyes. It was worth a try.

I was right about Sandy and Helen. A few weeks later, I was waiting for the lift, and as the doors opened I could see they were entwined in each other's arms and oblivious to the rest of the world – it is pleasing to report that they have been happily married for over fifty years.

After a while, I was allowed to take simple emergency cases such as appendectomies, suturing and the dressings of burns with the young, also inexperienced, house surgeon. I felt I had scaled the heights as I handed Garfield Davies the scalpel and our eyes met over our masks. These relatively simple operations were light-hearted affairs, and innocent flirting was commonplace, fun and entirely acceptable. I was teased unmercifully about my tanned back as ice cubes were dropped unceremoniously through the taped openings of my green gown, and the placing on the back of my neck of freezing ether swabs was another favourite ploy. On one occasion, I chased the joker, who calmly stuck his foot out and I tumbled onto the concrete floor, writhing in short-lived agony and collecting an impressive bruise; but it was a good laugh.

We had a considerable assortment of emergency cases during the night: some were quite simple, others very complicated. There were road accidents and knife accidents; one was a Smithfield butcher who had severed his femoral artery with his butcher's cleaver. Later, I was to hear of an unexpected "find" when another young butcher was admitted. He hadn't been wearing the obligatory heavy leather protection, and a knife had gone straight into his groin as he was filleting meat, severing an artery. The Theatre Sister was on hand and reported, 'Whilst pressure was being applied to his gushing wound, I cut off his jeans and found £1,000 in blood-soaked notes in his back pocket.'

The practical Sister calmly washed the treasure trove, note by note, under the cold tap. She then put them in the heated cabinet to dry and returned the now unsullied notes to the rightful (or possibly not rightful) grateful owner.

I saw my first skin grafting whilst I was working on theatres. The skin was taken from a man's leg and grafted onto his forearm. Apparently, the patient had been drunk and had fallen asleep on his bed and had woken up to the smell of his own flesh being burnt by a nearby electric fire – he managed to get back to the pub for some Dutch courage before coming to hospital.

An emergency "ten-minute" Caesarean operation was a highlight of my time in theatres and gave me my first opportunity to see the miraculous birth of a slimy, blue, but simply beautiful baby girl. At the same time, there were emergency operations on tiny premature babies with little or no chance of survival, which were overwhelmingly distressing.

I enjoyed the company of a ninety-year-old man, who had been admitted with a strangulated hernia and, in view of his age, it had been decided to carry out his operation under local anaesthetic. We had been expecting a weak and worried patient but instead found a very alert, high-spirited cockney who had lived all his life in the East End of London and had only recently retired from working at the Arsenal football ground. I held the old man's wrinkled and heavily veined hand in case he was frightened. It was clear, though, that he was enjoying being the centre of attention, and he regaled us with one story after another until the last stitch had been sewn. He was a breath of fresh air, and we were so sorry to learn that the old chap died suddenly on Fleet Street Ward two days later.

We had our share of sad cases, too. I had always found it hard to comprehend the sordid events one read about in the newspapers relating to criminal abortions, until one day a thirty-one-year-old woman arrived with us, having attempted a self-induced abortion when she had become pregnant by a man who was not her husband. Her husband, who had been away in the navy, agreed they should remain together but only if she got rid of the baby. We couldn't save the poor woman; she died a dreadful, inevitable death from gas gangrene, leaving her three other children with no mother.

Some nights we worked non-stop from 7.30pm until 8am without a break, and I wondered how the surgeons managed on so little rest when they had to work the following day. On busy nights, we frequently only managed to get by on a cup of soup, cornflakes, and bread and butter, which we grabbed when we had a minute.

Miss Ormiston was worried that so many theatre nurses were feeling unwell: so much so that, in true Ormi fashion, she provided a bottle of multi-vitamins in each operating theatre for us all to take. 'Nurse Tisdale, you are to take two tablets twice a day and don't forget!' I didn't take even one tablet. I was about to leave theatres for good; and anyway, I had something else on my mind. I had a plan which, if I wasn't caught, would give my parents a shock and cause them some amusement. I took off my greens for the last time and surreptitiously secreted them in a laundry bag which I put under my arm and innocently went off duty and caught the train home. It was nearly midnight and my parents were on their way to bed when I became the gowned and masked interloper. They were flabbergasted. I had achieved my objective and they had greatly enjoyed the ruse. There is no doubt they were impressed, but I'm not sure whether this was due to my theatricals or their amazement at my daring to borrow the greens from right under Belinda's nose.

To my surprise, I found I had to work on theatres again for several days before going to Rahere Ward. This was to my advantage – I was able to return the "stolen" items without difficulty, and nobody ever found out what I had been up to.

Chapter Nine

Puzzles and Pieces of Soap

A bald, bespectacled, fully dressed patient was sitting by his bed as I reported for duty on Rahere Ward. The gentleman was wearing a smart dark suit, a freshly laundered white shirt with a stiff detachable collar, cuffs fastened with gold cufflinks and an understated, obviously expensive, floral silk tie. He looked the epitome of good taste and elegance and was likely, I thought, to be a "pillar of society". Mr Medcalf suffered from diabetes and had been a patient on Rahere Ward for several days and was now waiting to be discharged, after which he was planning to go straight back to work in the City.

Unexpectedly, a torrent of slurred swear words poured from his mouth, and he began to sweat profusely and became increasingly confused and aggressive – typical symptoms, I realised, of a too-low blood sugar. This was not good news either for him or for me. He adamantly refused a glucose drink and needed an intravenous infusion.

I struggled to remove the gentleman's jacket. I struggled to undo his cufflinks, and I struggled to roll up his sleeve to reveal a suitable vein, but Mr Medcalf was having none of it. He suddenly spied a nearby tea trolley on which sat a delicious Victoria Sandwich cake, with its tempting raspberry jam and glistening white icing. He released himself from my clasp, leapt up, pinched a piece of cake and took a large bite. His urgency to eat the forbidden confectionery blessedly pushed up his blood sugar, and within minutes his aggression waned. He no longer required the emergency intravenous dextrose. His recovery was rapid and remarkable.

I came to know Mr Medcalf quite well as the months went by. He was charming and indeed a pillar of society. He remembered nothing of our first encounter or his dramatic conduct. I learnt that first impressions of unusual behaviour are worthy of note, and I learned there's nothing quite like a banned Victoria Sandwich.

Sister Rahere, for some reason, reminded me of Beatrix Potter's Mrs Tittlemouse. She was small in stature and fastidious as she scuttled about her duties with her eyes darting in every direction looking for any sign of untidiness. Sister made up for her diminutive build by shouting when roused and under pressure, but it was generally all bluster, and she was unusually quick to apologise to her nurses after she had calmed down.

Whilst I worked on Rahere, I was nicknamed "Smiler" by the patients, which I rather liked, but the smile was wiped off my face on the occasion Sister bitterly accused me of mislaying a needle that I knew had been taken away by the syringe service woman. On realising her mistake, she and I parted the best of friends, and she wished what was "left of me" a good day off. Later, to my horror, I remembered I had overlooked signing the drug book, but on my return she appeared to have forgotten my misdemeanour and she never mentioned the unforgivable sin.

New pieces of equipment on the wards were few and far between, but a new "state-of-the-art" bed had been set in place on a nearby ward and was causing a stir. The innovative bed had handles that wound up the top and the foot of the mattress, thus making three sections. The Sister trying out the gadgetry was delighted with her new toy and gathered her nurses round to demonstrate how the system worked. She took off her cuffs, rolled up her sleeves and started winding. In the bed was a very large cockney lady who had heart failure, and, unfortunately, halfway through the display Sister trapped the patient's generous buttocks between the mattresses, at which point the patient yelled, 'Sister, you're pinching me arse!' The prim and proper Sister wouldn't have hurt a fly, let alone a patient, and was mortified. We never found out whether she, or any other Sister for that matter, ordered any of these beds with their new-fangled, bottom-pinching adjustments.

*

We were a happy team on Rahere and had the benefit of a lovely Irish ward maid with a charming accent called Maureen. She had worked on the ward for many years and was wedded to the hospital. She regaled us with many a story, including one about a stunning nurse who was nicknamed *Forever Amber* (the name of a romantic novel which was turned into a film in 1947). Apparently, Amber was highly popular with the medical students and doctors; she was also a very good tennis player and a dab hand with the needle. Due to the rationing of clothes, which was still in place after the war, she set about making her own stylish apparel, including her own fashionable white tennis outfits. This approach was to be applauded, and her handiwork was much admired until one day the very strict Home Sister carried out a raid on Amber's bedroom, where she found one of the cream linen curtains from a ward screen laid out on Amber's bed, already cut out as tennis shorts. Amber had to go. She was dismissed immediately, never to be seen again, which everyone agreed was a pity as she was reputed to be a wonderful nurse.

*

The patients on the ward came from a wide spectrum of society. They varied from a senior executive at BOAC (British Overseas Airways Corporation), who said he would fix me up with a job as an air hostess any time I wished, to a sad, little man called Mr Fox who came from the squalid slums of the East End where he had no bath and only an outside privy. The poor old chap couldn't bend down to tie his shoelaces, and for many months he had worn the same socks continuously, even in bed. His feet were filthy and smelt like ripe Munster cheese. He knew he was dirty and smelly and said if he had known he was coming to hospital, he would have gone to the public baths at Goulston Square in Whitechapel first. I soaked and soaped the indescribably grimy feet before tackling his thick, horny toenails. This was all in a day's work, and what better way to get to know the patient than over a dirty pair of feet? The dirt and smell were insignificant and unavoidable in his situation; it was the man below the grime that mattered, and that was what I had now begun to understand.

It was always difficult to come back after a day off, but this was tempered by the welcome back we received from the long-stay patients and their families. Mr Martin, who suffered from terminal cancer, was an example of the bond between the patient and the nursing staff. The gratitude and pleasure he gave us in return for the care we gave him was unequalled. The poor man was dreadfully incontinent, and time and again we would hear his soft voice whispering apologetically that he thought he had "done it in the bed again" just after we had cleaned him and changed and replaced his sheets with fresh linen yet again. On the morning he died, he managed to sit up in bed and thank us warmly for all we had done – it was the patients who made our job so worthwhile.

Mr Martin's wife came to visit us shortly after his funeral, bearing an unexpected gift of a basket full of individually tied little bunches of delicate and sweet-smelling violets – one for each nurse who had looked after him. We were all incredibly touched by her thoughtful gesture.

For the first time, I was made fully responsible for laying out a patient. Mr Reider, who had stomach cancer, was an elderly gentleman of German origin who had been going downhill fast; but in his own estimation, this wasn't fast enough. He was unmarried and alone in the world and never had visitors. He would cheerfully announce he was quite ready to die and that he might just as well go, as we all had to sometime. He lingered on longer than he would have liked, but subsequently he died a peaceful death. I was detailed to perform the last offices with a junior nurse as my assistant. I collected the necessary equipment and managed a wry smile as I remembered being told about a nurse who had asked Sister if shrouds were washable.

My assistant was naturally apprehensive; it was the first time she had helped with the procedure and she needed reassurance. I reminded her that whilst Mr Reider was alive, there was nothing she wouldn't do for him, and this last service we were offering was no different from the others.

When we had completed our final duty, we opened a nearby window and put a posy of flowers on Mr Reider's locker. I then recollected Miss Davies's advice when we were at PTS: 'Stand back and be critical of your endeavours; but also take pleasure in the results of the task you have completed.' We both agreed we had done a good job. Mr Reider looked peaceful and serene. He would have been well pleased.

*

Remembrance Sunday was on 13th November, and several of us volunteered to sell poppies outside the Main General Post Office, which was next door to the hospital. We started at 6am to catch the postal sorters as they came off their night shift from the Mount Pleasant Sorting Office, and off we went in the dark and cold, wrapped warmly in our navy cloaks. We pinned one of the traditional red poppies firmly onto our cloaks, perched our caps prettily on our heads and hung the trays of poppies round our necks. We rattled the collection tins and the sixpenny pieces poured in. How could the postmen possibly resist us? They couldn't, and we raised a goodly amount for the Earl Haig Poppy Fund.

The Lord Mayor's Show was held on the same bitter day. This grand annual event celebrating the City's heritage was always held on the second Saturday of November and continues to this day. In my three hours off duty and still wearing my uniform, I slipped out to join the crowds watching the parade by St Paul's Cathedral. I saw Sir Bernard Waley Cohen, the new Lord Mayor, looking very magisterial in his scarlet robe and his feathered black tricorn hat, as he sat in his gold, ornately decorated coach, which was being pulled by six magnificent horses. He leaned out of the open side of the carriage and gave me a special wave, or so I thought, until I saw him do exactly the same to others standing nearby.

We learnt that wearing our uniform in the City paid dividends, although we were not allowed to go beyond a certain radius of the hospital. St Paul's Cathedral was well within our limits, and one wintry December afternoon, Meg and I, in full regalia, decided to visit the cathedral and its Whispering Gallery. In 1960, there was no admission fee to the cathedral, although payment was required from those wishing to climb to the gallery; but for us

St Paul's Cathedral.

it was free. We were confident that the ascent would be easy. We were, after all, used to being on our feet all day, but our optimism lessened the farther up we climbed; the treads on the winding stone staircase were worn, uneven and narrow, and the 257 steps to the base of the dome felt like 200 steps too far.

St Paul's Cathedral, designed by the famous architect Sir Christopher Wren, was built between 1675 and 1710, and the Whispering Gallery, at the base of the iconic dome, acquired its name due to a quirk in the construction of the building which was an accidental by-product of the architectural design. This peculiarity allows a whisper made against its walls to be audible on the opposite side of the gallery. We made our magical whispers and then made our way down and back on duty. Well worth the effort, we agreed, but not for the fainthearted.

Back on the ward, I found we had admitted a very sick patient who was of the Roman Catholic faith and whose family had asked that he should be given the last rites. When the priest arrived, we were busy with the patient and had to keep him waiting for a few minutes. Suddenly the priest could contain himself no longer and blurted out, 'I wish they would hurry up. I want to get back in time to see *Wagon Train* on the television.'

I was at a loss for words and couldn't wait to tell the tale to my close Roman Catholic friends Anna and Anne.

In mid-December, Beth came back from her home in Banwell, Somerset, to see Dr Oswald, the TB specialist. She appeared to be a picture of health and was looking forward to her three months' "holiday" in a hotel in Davos – we agreed it was a good time to be on the ski slopes.

It was not such good news for another member of our set who managed to slip, fall and break a bottle of blood and sever an artery, nerve and tendon in her wrist. This was bad on two accounts. Firstly, we all felt guilty because we hadn't realised it was her birthday; and secondly, she was likely to be off sick for some time. The first was quickly rectified when we bought her a cotton fresh, rosebud print nightdress, and the second may have been a blessing in disguise as nursing was not really to her liking, and this was the perfect excuse for her to leave forever.

*

Christmas was drawing ever closer. It was no secret that most of us chose to work over the festive period, and this would be the first hospital Christmas I had experienced. Everywhere began to bustle with activity. Pianos, one for each ward, were lined up in the main hospital corridor, and an abundance of Christmas trees were due to arrive in the Square. Parties were beginning to herald the fun, and a group of girls, who arrived back after midnight, sought the help of a sergeant from nearby Snow Hill Police Station, who obliged by lifting them, one by one, over the mortuary gates.

I was sent off by Sister to buy eighteen puzzles, eighteen pieces of soap and eighteen combs for the men's stockings. I hoped her calculations were correct as we had twenty-six beds, but who was I to challenge her? The anticipation of a hospital Christmas was truly thrilling. I could hardly wait.

Chapter Ten

Christmas and the Grosvenor

Word soon got around that the Christmas trees had arrived in the Square. What a pantomime! The Sisters were off – sleeves rolled up, sleeves rolled down, cuffs in place (or not), flowing muslin caps askew and blue dresses hitched above the knee. It was a sight to savour. The tall, dark and beautiful Sister Waring (Miss Walker) was first on the scene. She had the longest legs and her ward was on the ground floor, giving her a distinct advantage. Once satisfied with her choice, she tied a large label, WARING WARD, around the trunk of the best-shaped tree. Our Sister Rahere didn't fare quite so well, although we too were on the ground floor. Her little legs wouldn't carry her fast enough, which wasn't surprising as she was old enough to be the winner's mother.

By Christmas Eve there was a mad rush to finish the decorations. Every ward had a different theme; and patients, ex-patients, medical students, nurses and the consultants' wives all lent a hand to compete for the best decorated ward in the hospital. Unfortunately, there was no one on Rahere Ward who was artistically minded, and our display was predictably obvious. Still, we were undeterred by our lack of artistry, and a brightly coloured decoration was placed on each patient's locker, and silver tinsel was hung over each bed and also placed on the windowsills. Large balloons were hung in clusters at the entrance to the ward, and lurid multi-coloured paper streamers, made by the patients, were hung wall-to-wall. The decorated Christmas tree with its fairy lights, glass baubles and a fairy on the top was a delight to behold. Back then, there were no concerns about fire hazards.

I had a moment of panic when it was suggested I should design the decoration to be attached to our caps. This was not a good idea, and I was soon relieved of the duty. Prickly holly, tiny silver bells and mistletoe were stitched onto a wide band of scarlet ribbon, which was then sewn onto the band of our caps. I was banished from the Sewing Bee, but a kind volunteer fashioned mine, and in the end we were pleased with our (their) efforts. I would be lying if I said we won the competition for the best dressed cap, but at least the mistletoe proved to be a success.

Chocolates and bottles of wine arrived on the ward and, surprisingly, so did two patients who had been discharged earlier in the year. They had been invited to stay over the Christmas period as they were known to be without family or friends. They were with us for four days and appeared to thoroughly enjoy every minute of their stay. I had a problem, though – I had only bought eighteen pieces of soap and eighteen puzzles and the addition of these extra gentlemen took our number to twenty-three. As expected, I was sent off to make up the deficit and to add a few extra goodies for the men's stockings. The gifts were given to Sister for her to wrap and fill all the stockings. The night nurses fulfilled the role of Father Christmas and hung a stocking at the foot of each patient's bed. We were told that everything was paid for by individual ward funds and Barts' charitable funds and nothing by the National Health Service.

We were given a Christmas Eve tea party by Sister Rahere and Sister Colston [Miss Way], who was a saintly individual, known to have exquisite silk underwear, from the female ward opposite. This was held in the corridor area between the two wards. Rahere (the men's ward) and Colston (the women's) together constituted what was referred to as the "firm" as both wards shared the same consultants. All the nurses and medical students were served by the Sisters, who refused all offers of help – we were not allowed to lift a finger. Then it was back to the ward for the evening duties before taking part in the customary carol singing.

We assembled in the Great Hall, which was a treat as most of the time it was out of bounds to mere student nurses. Its spectacular entrance and grand staircase had, along with all the wards and other buildings, been designed by James Gibbs in the eighteenth century when there was a complete rebuild of the hospital. Two large dramatic paintings hanging on the staircase caught my eye, and I discovered that they were painted in the 1730s by the famous William Hogarth, the father of satirical caricature. I had never heard of the artist but even I

"The Pool of Bethesda" one of the paintings on the Great Hall staircase by Hogarth.

could see that the paintings in front of us were not caricatures. Apparently, Hogarth wanted to demonstrate that an English artist could excel both at the grand historical style of painting and devotional paintings that depicted care and healing. *The Good Samaritan* portrayed a traveller, who, after being beaten and robbed, is saved not by two holy men passing by, but by a Samaritan, from a despised race, who stopped and cared for him. However, it was the other painting, called *Christ at the Pool of Bethesda,* which interested me most. It is thought that Hogarth used patients from the wards as models and also as a teaching aid for the trainee physicians so they could attempt to diagnose the various conditions depicted, which seemed such a good idea.

There was something very special about taking part in the long-held custom of carol singing throughout the whole hospital, and we vied with each other to take part. Our cloaks were reversed to reveal their scarlet linings, and we processed from the Great Hall down the staircase and across the Square holding our lit lanterns aloft. The wards were prepared for us, and the ward lights had already been dimmed and the candles lit on all the patients' lockers. Our lanterns glowed as we processed around both sides of every ward, and the

Gathering on the staircase before carol singing around the hospital.

patients and staff alike were touched and tearful. There can be few sights more emotive than listening to the singing of carols by candlelight, performed by fresh-faced uniformed young nurses. After a final short prayer at each port of call, we moved on to the next venue. Our final carol was performed outside Snow Hill Police Station, where we recovered our equilibrium and were entertained to coffee and assured of continued support when climbing over the mortuary gate – at any time of the night. We made our way to All Souls, Langham Place, in Marylebone for midnight communion where there was a huge congregation, many of whom were uniformed nurses from various London hospitals. We were in mufti as we were out of our permitted radius, and it never occurred to us to disobey this strict rule. All Souls was full of young students and was led by the renowned chaplain to the Queen, the charismatic rector the Revd John Stott, who was robed in his scarlet cassock. This handsome, relatively young man was much sought after by the fairer sex but to the disappointment of many remained a lifelong celibate. Then it was back to the hospital for present-opening with friends in Anne's room. The gifts exchanged mainly consisted of bars of soap, toothpaste and Polos. We then went to bed at 3.30am for three hours' sleep before the big day.

Merry Christmas! I dragged myself out of bed and cursed the truly awful 6.20am wake-up bell, which was being rung incessantly up and down the corridor. Bleary-eyed, I dressed and put on my beautifully decorated cap before going down to breakfast, muttering Christmas greetings to all on my way. A sustaining meal of bacon, egg and tomato prepared me for a heavy day ahead with no official off-duty period.

Sister Rahere had already been on duty for some time and was looking rather comical in her over-decorated cap. The patients were, or at least appeared to be, delighted with their Christmas stockings; notably, of course, with the pieces of soap and the puzzles. Many had not received presents for a long time, and some had never before received a stocking or even knew of the tradition.

Sister had already moved two of the very sick patients into side rooms to ensure peace and quiet. We were assigned to take it in turns to carry out their care and to look after their relatives throughout the day. It was a difficult time for them, and the celebration of Christmas must have been a poignant occasion.

There were Christmas greetings for all the patients and a special hug for the very old men, those aged eighty or more, as we asked them whether they would prefer a boiled or scrambled egg. We cooked breakfast for the patients every weekend and on bank holidays, and today was no exception. I don't think we managed the toast to go with the scrambled egg, but no one seemed to mind, and the bread and butter had been carefully prepared to perfection, cut into crustless triangles by the junior night nurse. On this morning of goodwill, we managed to muddle the orders, but there were no complaints.

An early special Christmas Dinner in the Nurses' Dining Room was a treat; all the tables were laid up with white damask cloths and colourful crackers. We were served at our seats by Molly, who usually grumbled and bossed us around as she dished up food from a counter, but on this occasion she managed to be moderately civil. There was melon followed by turkey with the traditional stuffing, bread sauce, bacon rolls and sausages. Christmas pudding, mince pies and fruit rounded off the feast. I looked around the dining room to enjoy the moment. It truly was a wonderful sight as every nurse was bedecked in her decorated cap.

The best bit of the day came next when about a hundred and fifty nurses left the dining room and went into the Square. It was here we linked arms to encircle the fountain and sang A*uld Lang Syne*. At the finale of our magnificent rendition, a Father

The surgeon serving out the Christmas pudding with Sister's help.

Christmas was spied leaving the children's ward, who, on closer inspection, could be seen to be the popular anaesthetist Malcolm Evans. This was too good an opportunity to miss, and quick as a flash he was grasped, two nurses to a limb, and swung to and fro at the mercy of the decorated "angels", before he was thrown headlong into the fountain. He emerged drenched but smiling with his white beard missing and his red costume now a shade of pink, whilst the water under the fountain had turned into a crimson lake. Sir James Patterson Ross was walking across the Square at the same time and was heard to say that he had never seen such a spectacular sight in all his time at the hospital.

At 1pm sharp, the consultants were ready for their performance. Attired in traditional pleated chefs' hats and lurid flowery aprons, they looked the part as they sharpened their carving knives with frightening expertise. Amid much applause and with a flourish of artistry and precision, the huge bird was anatomised. Vegetables, along with all the tasty trimmings, were arranged delicately on the plates, and the consultants' children served the patients. The Christmas pudding, with its sprig of holly, was lit with ease due to a liberal dousing of good quality brandy purchased specially, and was paraded round the ward for all to admire. (The hospital brandy given to patients for their medicinal needs was not used; apparently, it was so weak that ignition would be impossible.) The patients' wine glasses were recharged, and a happy, somewhat inebriated nap was welcomed.

There was no public transport on Christmas Day and many families didn't own a car, but those who were able to visit did so in the afternoon and enjoyed a slice of a large Christmas cake which had been made and then iced and piped by the chefs in the hospital kitchens. Each cake had a different design and was adorned with multiple gaudy ornaments. The chefs did us proud.

We visited other wards to view their decorations, but none surpassed Waring Ward which was, as usual, the best – they always went to town on their themes. Sister Waring, now in her late eighties, recalls when one of her themes was the popular television programme *To the Manor Born* with Penelope Keith as the aristocratic lady living in a country mansion. One of their long-stay patients, a builder by trade known as Hickey the Brickey, had taken charge and had made a very authentic fireplace suitable for the "Manor". The consultant surgeon and his family that year turned up on Christmas Day all dressed in smart hunting pink and were a sight to behold.

After over twelve hours on duty, we were all ready to drop, and I, for one, was glad to be residing in Queen Mary's Nurses' Home and was able to fall into bed without delay. This wasn't the case for the three nurses who missed the coach back to Maybury Mansions, the nurses' hostel in the West End. In their naivety, they didn't realise there were no trains on Christmas Day. Disconsolate at the prospect of a very long walk, they stood forlornly by the underground station rapidly losing their Christmas spirit until a taxi drew up and offered them a free ride. Their joy was revived, and all was well that ended well.

The medical students were the lucky ones. They collapsed into the temporarily erected beds in the pathology labs on each floor and the next morning, were woken by a "nice early morning cup of tea" by the night nurse to clear their obligatory sore heads. A hurried departure was made before the arrival of Sister, although everyone tended to turn a blind eye during the festive season.

We were still celebrating on Boxing Day. This was the day for the medical students to perform the infamous ward shows, which were usually pretty bad and under-rehearsed, but greatly enjoyed in spite of the jeering from other competing firms. The shows provided an opportunity to poke fun at their mentors without fear of recrimination. For many medical students, the Christmas ward shows were the high point of the academic year. The tradition was for each "firm" to produce a peripatetic show that could be presented around the various wards on Christmas Day and Boxing Day; but this year, as Christmas was on a Sunday, which was deemed a day not for theatricals, they took place on Boxing Day and on the 27th. The best ward show was put on by the boys from the Outpatients' Department who did a skit using the music from *West Side Story* composed by Leonard Bernstein, taking the song *America* and changing it to *Tight as a Tick at the Grosvenor*.

It was obvious that it was not what you knew but *who* you knew when it came to the provision of props. Apparently, one year, three medical students danced a frenzied "Can Can" resplendent in costumes supplied from the wardrobe of the Royal Opera House, generously loaned because the head of their firm, Professor Scowen, was its honorary physician. Another year, London Zoo obliged by coming up trumps with a parrot for a pirate's shoulder. This was grand until the raucous bird woke all and sundry in the students' hostel at dawn each morning.

In 1960, Graham Chapman, who became a well-known member of the hugely successful Monty Python comedy team, arrived on the scene to undertake his clinical studies. He had read medicine at Cambridge where he had been a member of the Footlights Club, and he had an immediate effect on the quality of Barts drama. He transformed the Christmas Pot Pourri show, which was an amalgamation of all the best bits of the ward shows, and made it into a complete evening's entertainment at the Cripple Gate Theatre. The usual amateurish assembly of rudery and ham was turned into elegance and wit. Whilst Chapman was at Barts, he managed to continue his comedy writing and performing and amazingly was able to persuade the Dean to allow him to take a year off to go on a world tour with John Cleese and Tim Brooke-Taylor. To everyone's surprise, he did return to complete his studies and qualify, although he never practised. On his death in 1989, one of his fellow students, Alan Bailey, remembered him as one 'who brought the art of medicine into his life and dealings with his fellow men and whose untimely death left the world duller than it was before.'

*

Our Christmas frivolity wasn't over yet. There was Matron's "amazing" Christmas Party in the hospital to attend, which was, as expected, an extremely boring affair and certainly not in any way frivolous. However, much better was the thought of her Ball, which she was to give us at the Grosvenor House Hotel on 4th January. The medical students became increasingly attentive in the hope they would receive an invitation. We kept them guessing – lovely girls, free dinner and drink and a first-class band; what more could they want?

With my father's usual financial assistance, I bought a very pretty, daring strapless dress. It was a creation in organza, with pink and white candy stripes with gold thread woven into the white stripes, and it had a voluminous full skirt. To provide the last touch of elegance, I borrowed a delicate string of pearls from my mother to wear round my neck. Unlike the May Ball at Oxford, when I had mistakenly thought I was appropriately attired, this time I was determined to dress to befit the occasion. On the day of the Ball, Anna and I went off to be pampered. We had decided on John Cornells, not just because it was a smart hairdressing salon but because it had greatly discounted prices as it was the beginning of the week. Not for us a quick shampoo and set in the Nurses' Home. No, it was to be the real McCoy. Neither of us had ever had a manicure before, and this was to be a short-lived extravagance as we knew the delicious shiny pink nail polish would have to be removed before we went back on duty.

The new "beehive" hairstyle came next. For this to be successful, our hair had to be wound round up-to-the-minute, very large rollers, before being dried under a hair dryer for half an hour. The "comb out" was performed by our now close friend John and was another lengthy process. He took strands of our hair which he then vigorously backcombed into a large bouffant. At last, we were both done to perfection. We felt a million dollars as we left the salon; in fact, not like nurses at all, which reminded me that a patient's relative had called me Miss the other day and was firmly reprimanded by the patient who said, 'She is not a Miss; she's a nurse.'

We had plenty of time for the finishing touches. Anna was going to look very glamorous in her pale blue three-quarter length satin dress, on which she was planning to pin a corsage of carnations, and her matching stilettos – both of which were chosen with impeccable taste. We were due to meet our escorts at 9pm, and at 8.55, as a final task, I zipped Anna into her gown. Snap! The teeth on the zip had separated to reveal a long, large and seemingly irreparable gap. 'What have you done? That's it. I can't possibly go,' she shrieked. The cry of anguish could be heard down the corridor and, as if by magic, a practical pro arrived with her sewing kit and with tiny, exquisite and invisible stitches sewed Anna into her gown. Tears mopped up, make-up restored, corsage pinned on – we were only five minutes late.

Meanwhile, Paula – the dark-haired beauty of our set – had managed to pull off an excellent deal. 'I had absolutely nothing suitable to wear until yesterday,' she declared, 'and then a nurse on the ward mentioned that a year ago she had left a long pink satin dress at the dry cleaner's and said if I wanted to pay 25/- to collect it, it was mine.' Well, Paula did as she was bid, and although, on her own admission, she slightly popped out of the top of it, she still managed to steal the show.

The invitees arrived, impeccably dressed in their dinner jackets and looking pleased with themselves. They were under the impression they had been chosen for their individual charm and good looks, but this was not strictly true. We had decided to go in a group rather than be "coupled-up", but each nurse had to apply for two tickets, so it appeared as though we had individual beaus. Anthony Balfour, a fourth-year medical student, was on my ticket. My brother Paul, who was not a medical student, came down from Warwickshire at Anna's invitation.

The Grosvenor House Hotel in Park Lane was imposing. Apparently, it had been one of the residences of the 1st Duke of Westminster who had a link, albeit a tenuous one, to the hospital. In 1887, together with one of our own famous surgeons, Sir James Paget, the Duke had been appointed a trustee of the Queen Victoria Jubilee Institute of Nurses. The institute was founded to

My brother with me on the left and Anna on the right.

provide trained nurses to the sick poor, and Sir James took the greatest interest in the institute and was present at Windsor Castle when her Majesty received the "Queen's Nurses" in 1897. The institute has thrived over the years and to this day continues to support district nurses and other nurses working in the community.

I was very familiar with Park Lane for no other reason than it was the second most valuable property on the Monopoly board game, and when a red wooden hotel was "bought" and placed on the board, it assured the player of almost certain success. The Grosvenor House Hotel, of course, was not a red wooden hotel – it was majestic and appropriate for the very grand occasion.

We were not accustomed to such grandeur, but it was an annual event for Matron. She stood at the entrance to the ballroom looking very elegant in her long black gown and immaculate gloves as she greeted us royally and shook us by the hand. I couldn't resist my usual slight bob.

A five-course dinner was served, which included soup, a fish dish, a main meat course and a sickly pudding with cheese to finish. A silver ice bucket, in which chunks of ice chilled the white wine, had pride of place on the table and was replaced, as required, with a full bottle by the efficient wine waiter. I remember little about the dancing apart from the last waltz. Anthony Balfour had gone missing – he had probably found another belle – and I was asked to dance by a rather dashing Scot in a swinging kilt called Stewart who spoke with a broad Scottish accent, and I didn't understand a word he said. No prospects there, I decided.

The Ball ended. It was time for the twelve of us to go for a late-night coffee. Having had a taste of the high life, and as we were dressed for the part, we thought a smart place would be appropriate. This was ridiculous. The one we found to our liking was far too expensive. Second stop: Euston Station, but the café was closed. Finally, we ended up in Micks's Café in Fleet Street, which was cheap and awash with printers – we certainly added some glamour to their morning.

Arriving back at the hospital at 3.30am, we were surprised the porter let us in without a murmur, and Anna and I made our way to see Priscilla, who had not gone to the Ball but had worked until the early hours to cover for a party-goer. She was sad as she had just broken up with her long-standing boyfriend, and I don't imagine we helped much as we gave her a twirl in our ball gowns. I eventually crawled into bed at 4.30am and had two hours of blissful oblivion.

This wasn't quite the end of the memorable evening at the Grosvenor. Gayle had finally decided she had had enough of nursing but, being Gayle, she couldn't resist going to the Ball for a final fling before she left. She was due back on night duty at 2.30am, although unbeknown to any of us she did a moonlit flit and was gone for good.

Chapter Eleven

The Botany Mistress From Cheltenham Ladies' College

In the New Year, it was time to start our second-year study block. I was loath to leave the wards, but there were certainly fresh events in store. The new teaching department was very smart and was housed on the top floor of the new nurses' home. All the teaching rooms had a wonderful outlook over the city with a spectacular view of St Paul's Cathedral. Particularly noticeable were the large picture windows with Venetian blinds

The view of St Paul's Cathedral from the top floor of the new Nurses' Home.

which ran all along the corridor. In front of these were window boxes full of colourful displays of well-tended, unusual plants and flowers.

On our first day, we were greeted by Miss Winifred Hector, the Principal Sister Tutor. *Miss* Winifred Hector. Miss *Winifred* Hector, Miss Winifred *Hector* – whichever part of her name was emphasised, it always seemed to have a sniff of cleverness. To us she typified the academic nursing spinster – she wore very thick lensed glasses, and her uniform dress and apron almost reached down to her ankles (not for her the shorter skirt coming into fashion in the early 1960s, which, inch by inch, we were all adopting).

However, there was more to the veritable Miss Hector than met the eye, as we were to discover. Among her interests were natural history, sex and religion. More importantly, although we weren't aware of it at the time, she was to pioneer the future of nurses' training in Britain.

*

When Winifred Hector was seven, her mother, seeing the child's interest in local wildlife, spared the money to buy her a book called *Flowers for Children.* Later, Miss Hector would say that the gift had had a profound influence on her life as it laid the foundation for her abiding and absorbing interest in not only flowering plants, but also in ferns, birds and insects. Presumably, this explained the wonderful variety of British flora in the window boxes along the corridor of the teaching unit.

Winifred Hector's short sightedness was discovered when she found she couldn't read what was written on the blackboard, but once she was fitted out with glasses she started excelling in her class work. By the time she was eleven, she had gained a scholarship to Bishop Fox's Secondary School in Taunton where she was top in every subject, and this was followed by a scholarship to Bedford College London where she set her sights on becoming a Professor of Anglo Saxon. No mean aim for the daughter of an engine driver and parlourmaid.

After her first year at university, this outstanding student was dealt a blow when her eyesight became progressively worse and she required a frequent change in the prescription for her glasses, which her parents could ill afford. She was seen by a Harley Street specialist who immediately told her to stop reading. She was devastated. Reading was one of her great passions, but nevertheless his advice was heeded and her university course was reluctantly abandoned. She was determined not to give up, though, and gained another scholarship for the Somerset Farm Institute at Cannington where she studied poultry husbandry.

There were parts of the course she enjoyed, but the best thing was that there were boys in abundance. This was the first time Winifred Hector had met members of the opposite sex at close quarters, and she found them very interesting indeed. Still, the course was not to her liking – she had an aversion to killing hens and found the agricultural dirt distasteful.

Now nineteen, Winifred Hector was ready to make her own decision. She would be a nurse! She was sure that not much reading would be required in her new career; and her eyesight, although still very poor, was no longer deteriorating. Her GP extolled the value of training at a London teaching hospital and recommended St Bartholomew's. Without more ado, she set off for London in 1933 to face the highly regarded and strongly principled Christian Matron, Miss Helen Dey. The woman, looking splendid in her enormous white-winged army cap, black dress and white collar and cuffs, was awe-inspiring and wasted no time in telling the girl that she felt university women did not do well as nurses. Despite this inauspicious start, Winifred Hector's practical experience went in her favour – it was worth the neck-wringing of all those wretched hens – and she was offered a place.

She successfully completed her training but not before receiving a bad report for being argumentative. She was summoned to see the indomitable Miss Dey who pronounced, 'I think, Nurse Hector, you will be more successful as a Sister than as a probationer'.

The astute Matron was right, and after several years, Miss Hector became a junior Sister Tutor at the hospital under the watchful eye of the neat and self-possessed "old school" senior tutor Miss Fellows, who felt that all nurses should be hard-working, punctual, unfailingly kind, neat and well informed. All excellent qualities, but the new young Sister Tutor wanted more for her students.

She had been greatly influenced by what she had learned when she attended the Quinquennial Congress of the International Council of Nurses in the United States as far back as 1947. She listened to the American nurse teachers and was impressed by their willingness to experiment. This experience helped her to recognise the need to modernise nurse training in England and for nurses to receive education and not just training in physical tasks.

By the time of our second-year block in 1961, she had introduced many innovative reforms; her textbooks had become worldwide bestsellers, and in the late sixties she initiated the first nursing degree course in Britain between St Bartholomew's and City University. Thanks to her, for better or worse, the degree nurse had arrived. The degree was not without its detractors, and for many it was not necessarily a step forward. The days of the qualified nurse who had trained under the apprenticeship system would become a thing of the past, and nurses under training in the old system viewed the new graduate nurses with a jaundiced eye and often found them distant and uninvolved with the patients and less happy to carry out menial tasks.

*

From our youthful perspective, in the sixties, we thought that at the age of fifty, Miss Hector was far too old to even contemplate sex. How wrong we were. Our Principal Sister Tutor was not easily shocked by matters relating to sex, or for that matter male nudity; and indeed, as a fledgling tutor she had been incensed when she was prohibited by Miss Fellows from drawing diagrams of the male genito-urinary tract when she taught her nurses about prostatectomies. In her view, knowledge came before prudery.

She enjoyed recounting her first "meeting" with the male anatomy during the early days at her infant school when she had her first lesson from two little boys behind the school buildings when they showed her their infant organs and taunted her with not possessing one like them. When she was adolescent, she only had the haziest ideas of what was involved in sexual intercourse, and when a girl in her form had promised two boys that she would let them "do it" with her, Winifred Hector had no idea what she was talking about. Her mother never gave her any sex education except to say that when she left home she should be careful: 'Whatever that meant.'

One or two proposals of marriage came Miss Hector's way when she was young and more after she was sixty, but the astute woman felt this was because she was fairly well off and a good catch, and she had no difficulty in declining, realising that as a skilled nurse she was an attractive catch for an elderly man. She was astonished that men could possibly believe that a single woman would so want to be married that she would be prepared to devote her abilities and money to care for an elderly invalid. Winifred Hector was no fool.

In later life, she was twice approached about writing soft porn; this was perhaps due to her extensive writing on gynaecology. One of the proposers was an eminent physician who thought there was a big market in women's magazines for medical soft porn, and the other was from an acquaintance who wanted to write religious porn. To my surprise, Miss Hector wrote in her memoirs that she had been tempted, and that if she had been a quarter of a century younger when she had been approached, she might have agreed. Was this liberated lady really our spinster Sister Tutor?

Certainly, for all her apparent semblance of being a severe and serious individual, Winifred Hector had a dry sense of humour and was an excellent communicator. In front of the class she enjoyed "acting out" the juxtaposition of various organs in the abdominal cavity. When describing the female reproductive system, she described the whereabouts of the anatomical features with excitement and optimism. She selected a small nurse to stand before the class, and then behind the smaller individual she placed a somewhat taller nurse. With much drama, Miss Hector then stood behind the pair with her cloak spread wide and declared, '*You* are the bladder' (pointing to the front girl). '*You,* number two, are the uterus and *I* am the Fallopian tubes.' Her lessons were never to be forgotten, and her stories intermingled seamlessly with her lectures.

Winifred Hector kept us spellbound with her tales of her childhood exploits and her lately developed interest in geology and bryology (the study of mosses). When she went on holiday, she told us she never revealed where she worked or what she did. She took a delight, when asked, in saying that she was a teacher of natural sciences for which, of course, she was well qualified. When questioned more closely, she would admit to being the Botany Mistress from Cheltenham Ladies' College and over the years had never been caught out.

Among her admirers was the well-loved, then relatively unknown, local poet John Betjeman, who lived in a small house cluttered with books in Cloth Fair near Smithfield Meat Market and in the shadow of St Bartholomew the Great. He could often be seen wandering across the Square in an absent-minded manner, rumpled and fogeyish, and always wearing the same hat. He often visited Miss Hector in the Nursing School, and he and our revered Sister Tutor used to stand cosily and companionably together on the corridor of the eleventh floor looking out at the panorama of the city as he named every spire in sight and quoted endless verses of poetry.

Both Winifred Hector and John Betjeman were devoted Anglicans and frequently worshipped together at St Bartholomew the Great; on one occasion, he charmingly and gentlemanly gave up his kneeler to her when she found hers was missing and knelt happily on the hard stone floor, which she found most touching. According to Miss Hector's memoir, John Betjeman combined piety with a nagging uncertainty about the truth of Christianity and was deeply insecure. He had a dread, not exactly of death, but of being dead. It was this that led him to volunteer to visit the lonely, elderly male patients on Percivall Pott Ward where he was always made most welcome.

Later, Betjeman was to become not only a knight of the realm but also Poet Laureate and a television personality of some standing. When he was asked by the BBC to do a television series on his favourite sights of the City of London, naturally one of the places he chose was St Bartholomew's, and obviously he asked Miss Hector to take part. She prepared

John Betjeman enjoying a chat with his friend Winifred Hector.

herself carefully for the filming and duly turned up be suited, coiffed and camera-ready. Imagine her disappointment when she was sent off to change into her full uniform. When she reappeared, however, in resplendent blue and with her white starched veil floating down her back, all John Betjeman could utter respectfully was 'Oh Lor!' Only one take was required, and it would appear our venerable Principal Sister Tutor was a star in the making.

*

On one of my weekend visits home I was invited to a tea party at our local church's vicarage, but to my surprise I found I was the only guest. It was just me; the pleasant, bald vicar who was in his mid-forties and his charming eighty-year-old mother. A week after the event I received a forty-page letter from the said reverend with a proposal of marriage. To say I was astonished would be an understatement – I hardly knew the man, but I obviously must have passed muster with his mother.

I was sitting on my bed in my room reading and re-reading the tome when Meg arrived and saw me surrounded by sheets of writing paper on which were screeds of immaculate writing.

'What on earth is going on?' she demanded to know.

I replied calmly that I had just received a proposal of marriage.

'You *haven't*.'

'I have.'

'What are you going to do?'

'*Do*? Thank him very much but decline.' And off we went to supper.

*

Shortly before our time in Block came to an end, Miss Hector asked for volunteers to have a shot at writing a case history with a view to possible publication in a nursing journal. *Nothing lost, nothing gained,* I thought. What better story than that of Anne Tucker from Abernethy Ward and her new-found continence with her spout Elly. 'It would make a good yarn,' said Miss Hector, and I was granted permission to use Anne's case notes. It wasn't to be. I was told I was off to the dreaded mental hospital at Hill End St Albans and therefore couldn't take Anne's records with me – my thoughts of fame and authorship were thwarted.

Chapter Twelve

The Godforsaken Hospital

As we pulled up, it was already getting dark, and the taxi driver gave me a knowing look. 'Keep smiling,' he said, 'you'll soon get used to it.'

In front of me was a huge mental asylum; an old, sprawling, dismal, prison-like building with a towering chimney. I had yet to go inside the Victorian brick monstrosity, but I already dreaded the thought of working in a place like this and longed to be back in London.

I took a deep breath and entered what appeared to be an endless, unlit corridor. It was spine-chilling. Bats were flying above and they started swooping down repeatedly, only narrowly missing my head. Naturally, I ducked instinctively. Who wouldn't? After all, bats get in your hair, that's what bats *did*. This was not a good introduction to Hill End Hospital.

I made my way gingerly down the corridor and came upon an apparently inconsequential group of men and women who were walking relentlessly up and down. Up and down. Up and down. Others were standing alone, apparently frozen to the spot, and looking isolated and purposeless. One old woman was rocking backwards and forwards, banging her head against the wall; another marched down the corridor opening windows, followed almost immediately by a man who solemnly closed them all. It was perplexing until I realised it was the mentally sick patients who were parading. I also noticed that for them the bats were neither a disturbance nor a distraction.

The nurses' sleeping quarters were across the way in another crumbling building. My allocated space was on the ground floor in what had been a ward. The vast room, which had originally accommodated sixty patients, had been made into thirty cramped two-bedded cubicles that were separated only by a curtain. In the service of fairness and equality, red and black lines had been painted on the wooden floor. I had been allocated a place in a red zone and could see that my future roommate, in the black section, was well settled, judging by the piles of clothes on the floor and her unmade bed.

I had heard it said that some mothers cried when they saw the accommodation provided for their young student nurse daughters in this mental institution, and I was glad I was without my parents. One mother had taken a brief look and instantly taken her daughter away, saying, 'I wouldn't let a maid live in a place like this.'

The manorial life at Piggotts Manor, and even the relatively comfortable Queen Mary's Nurses' Home, had not prepared me for this. I could understand why Meg had been so upset and disappointed when she was told that her very first ward would be in her local run-down mental hospital.

My dismay was interrupted by the overtures of a friendly voice across the room. 'Welcome. You'll find it hard to believe at the moment, but it gets better, I promise you. It's just the initial shock,' she claimed. She went on: 'Cockroaches have a habit of crawling out of their hiding places in the dead of night. They are mainly in the bathroom and they creep out from round the pipes under the basin. We've tried a homemade bait of boric acid, white flour and white sugar without any success, and now we just try and bash them with a piece of wood, but as yet we have been outmanoeuvred.'

My face fell. 'What about the bats? I had to fight my way here.'

She laughed. 'You'll soon get used to them. They won't get in your hair; that's an old wives' tale, but they could target you with their droppings and they do have a habit of urinating all over the place.'

This was all *great* information for a newcomer, and there was more to come.

She continued: 'There are, of course, an abundance of mice, but they are field mice and rather sweet.' More bad news. I didn't relish a mouse invasion, whether they were of the field variety or otherwise. She added: 'I would suggest you avoid putting sweet papers in your wastepaper bin. And another thing: if you decide to have a bath in the bathroom above the Eye Ward, take heed. On one occasion a nurse left her undies in a hand basin and forgot to turn the taps off. Not only was the bathroom flooded, but the water had gone through the ceiling into the ward below. Most of the patients had had cataract surgery and had to lie very still, and so they lay motionless in their beds holding umbrellas over their heads until the floodwater subsided. It was a sight to be seen. There is some good news as far as the bathrooms are concerned; although they are decrepit and there are no bolts on the doors, you can have an excellent duo session. All of them have two, very deep, side-by-side baths which were used in the past for very disturbed patients. They are wonderful for tête-à-têtes.'

To give her credit, she was nothing if not thorough. Surely there could be no more? However, on she went.

'You will be constantly hungry; it's hard work here, and walking from one place to another takes a lot of energy. The remedy is the simple two-bar electric fire. You turn the fire on its back and then rest the food on the hot elements, and in no time at all you have a meal. Our favourites are soup, baked beans and toast. Good luck. Working at Hill End is an experience never to be forgotten.'

I felt I needed all the good luck in the world. Radios, apparently tuned into different stations, were blaring forth. Gramophones were playing favourite records – everything from *Living Doll* sung by Cliff Richard and *All Shook Up* by Elvis Presley to *Memories Are Made of This* by Dean Martin. Washed knickers and bras were strung up and drying over the rails of the cubicles. Most of the beds were unmade. I could see there would be no Maud or Amelia here to make our beds for us – it was our responsibility. I began to wonder whether I would ever feel at home here.

*

Hill End Hospital, St Albans, had been built for the mentally ill in 1900 and had originally housed one hundred male patients, many of whom had been transferred from prisons and were locked in. By 1937, the number of inmates – men *and* women – had increased to over 1,000. However, everything changed with the outbreak of war in 1939 and Barts moved almost lock, stock and barrel to the institution, and the mentally sick had to be transferred elsewhere at short notice. Although the hospital in London continued to maintain its general medical services and acted as a receiving and emergency clearing station for war casualties, including injured servicemen, patients requiring surgery were transported to Hill End to have their operations.

Five brisk, no-nonsense Sisters and eighteen of their nurses arrived undaunted, in the midst of bedlam, to set up a general hospital to cope with a large number of surgical cases in a very inadequate, ill-prepared mental institution. They found 1,000 beds made up of sixty bedded wards on two floors (with no lifts) and a number of padded "cells", as well as 1,000 crock hot water bottles (government issue), but little else.

There was only one small operating theatre which, together with other adjacent rooms and the very large barber's salon, had to be turned into three operating theatres to include anaesthetic and sterilising facilities. The large mirrors from the barber's shop were carefully put aside to be proudly reinstated on the walls after the war, when the barbers were back in business. As there was no gas on the wards, Primus stoves had to be used both for sterilising instruments, generally in fish kettles, and for cooking the food for all the patients.

Fortunately, only a small number of sick and injured servicemen were admitted to the hospital in the early days of the war, and there was relative calm. Then all hell let loose. Dunkirk was evacuated. In one week, over 600 servicemen were admitted to Hill End; and on one day, 321 battered, injured and exhausted men arrived in a single convoy. The operating theatre staff worked day and night, and the occupancy of the hospital rose to 1,000.

The Sister on the male plastic surgery ward during the war was none other than our Matron, the esteemed Miss Loveridge, who became a past master at dealing with situations which required a delicate touch. Apparently, one day, an American soldier had refused to sleep in the ward with a "nigger" and had tried his utmost to stab him with a pair of scissors; but ever the diplomat, Miss Loveridge gently suggested the black man should have the privilege of a side room, and all was well.

I was interested to learn that in 1944, Hill End had been chosen as one of the four main centres in the country to investigate the uses of penicillin. The bright yellow substance was injected painfully and with agonised precision, and the selected "lucky" patients ended up with bottoms like pincushions. Rumour had it that one moribund patient on the neurosurgical ward was on the point of death, but as a last resort he was injected with the miracle drug at three-hourly intervals throughout the night; and the next day, the "almost" dead patient was sitting up in bed eating his breakfast and enjoying a glass of beer!

During the dark days of the war, most of the training of student nurses took place at Hill End. Owing to wartime shortages and to save material, the uniform changed from long-sleeved dresses with stiff cuffs to short-sleeved dresses with soft collars and cuffs. The nurses carried their rations in their baskets: two ounces of butter, four of margarine and half a pound of sugar per week, plus a pound of jam or marmalade to last four weeks. The jam was often made of swede with pips and dye so it *looked* like raspberry jam, even if it didn't taste like it. Supper for the night nurses was invariably cheese, beetroot and slices of bread and margarine. Meagre as this may sound, it was apparently devoured as if it was a banquet – in those days, hunger was endless and rarely appeased.

Wartime night duty at Hill End was not without its excitement. The flying bombs, also known as buzz bombs, that had killed over 5,000 in London, were an interesting distraction. A third-year nurse at the time, Mary Penny, spoke of her experience one night when she was giving the night report to a junior colleague: 'We heard the buzz bomb coming our way, and as it got nearer and nearer, all the men flung their bedclothes over their heads. We, meanwhile, continued with the report. There was a very loud bang as the bomb exploded nearby, after which the men tentatively emerged to find us still sitting calmly at the table, dutifully completing the task before us.'

*

I, of course, back then knew little about what had happened in the war years at Hill End, but on my first night, I decided my sleeping arrangements were probably a fair imitation of what it had been like fifteen years earlier. I was extremely uncomfortable – the bed was narrow, the mattress was thin, and the girl sleeping next to me snored the hours away. I was also apprehensive about working on the neurosurgical ward, and I couldn't wait for the months to pass so I could leave.

The next day was cold and miserable – true February weather. With my head down and my cloak firmly around my shoulders, I rushed to get to the dining room for breakfast but lost my way in the maze of long corridors. Out of the gloom, a bicycle bell rang furiously, and I was lucky not to collide with one of the Night Sisters who was pedalling away for dear life on her way off duty. This method of transport appealed to me, but I was soon to learn that this was a forbidden pleasure for all student nurses, although it seemed to me to be an ideal way to cover the "miles" of corridors.

We didn't share our dining room with the psychiatric nurses, and I was soon to find out that the segregation was not just in the dining room but applied to all areas of the hospital. Our breakfast was served by the immaculately dressed Mrs Thacker, an Assistant Matron, who was wearing a wonderful lace cap with a bow under her chin. She was ably attended by Mavis, a Tynesider, dressed in rather grubby green overalls and who was known to say at *every* lunchtime, 'Plooms and coostard, Nurse?'

I arrived on Cavell Ward to find three nurses spreading damp tea leaves all over the floor. As I stared in disbelief, the young Sister – Miss Thomas – came on the scene and smiled at my incredulity, explaining, 'We save the damp tea leaves from the patients' breakfast every morning and scatter them over the old wooden floor before we sweep as it saves the dust from rising.

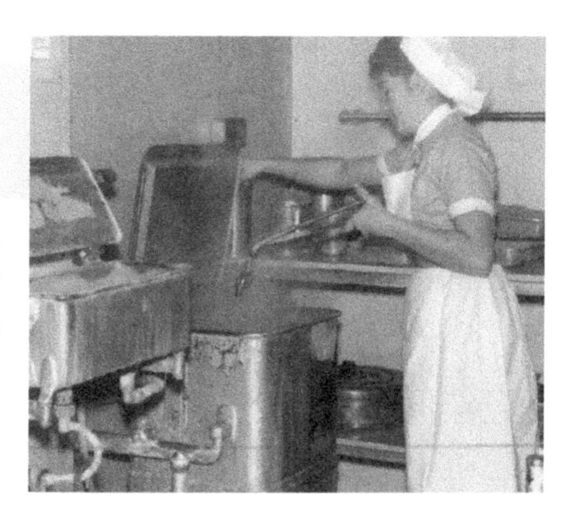
Dishing up bowls and instruments from the steamy steriliser.

You'll soon get used to our ways and our housework. We have little domestic help down here.'

At first, the ward appeared to have no particular semblance of order, but what was immediately noticeable was the cleanliness that was obviously due entirely to Sister Cavell and her nursing staff. There were men, women, children and babies on the ward, which surprised me. Some of them were up and dressed and walking around whilst others were being nursed in cubicles, and a fair number were comatose and close to death. We were very short of spare clothes for the children and were severely admonished by the Senior Registrar, Mr Hannigan, for allowing the infants to look messy and uncared for. Many of the patients had had their heads shaved and were awaiting their operations; other post-operative patients had beautifully bandaged heads, and I was glad I had learnt to master the capeline bandage at PTS.

I was now relatively senior, and as well as carrying out general nursing duties, I was told I was to be what was called "fifth" nurse and would therefore be responsible for sterilising all the instruments and equipment required on the ward, and I would also be in charge of laying up the craniotomy "sides". *Craniotomy sides?* I looked blank.

I was taken aside by Miss Kay, the Pink. 'Don't worry, it's not that difficult. If you remember; a craniotomy is where a disc of bone is removed from the skull, which allows the surgeon access to the brain underneath. After the operation, as to be expected, the patient is at great risk, and so a lot of different equipment is required to be on hand to monitor the patient when they return to the ward. All the post-operative craniotomy patients are "specialled" by a nurse because it's vital they have continuous observations and care.'

Several days passed without incident, and I was beginning to feel confident that I had mastered my new role. I was quietly satisfied with my proficiency, and several of my craniotomy sides had been used without complaint and occasionally with a compliment.

But suddenly my day changed from happy to horrid. I was humming away in the sterilising room as I went about my business when the pleasant Miss Kay (who was later to become a doctor) joined me. 'How are you getting on, Nurse Tisdale?' She inspected my work and was pleased to see the "sides" were expertly laid and murmured her approval. A minute later, I felt as if my life had fallen apart.

Miss Kay started checking the lumbar puncture sets which had been returned, as usual, to the ward by the operating theatre staff, and suddenly I saw her jaw drop. She could immediately see that they had not been autoclaved as the vents on the drums were still open. They had been returned without being sterilised and *I* had not noticed, and it was *my* responsibility to check them. I felt dreadful. Not only guilty, but extremely worried. I knew perfectly well that it was imperative that the sterilisation had to be carried out by the autoclave method so any spores were destroyed, but I also knew that several of the offending sets had already been used and may have infected the patients. I had failed and could be instrumental in causing the deaths of those under our care. This was undoubtedly the worst day since I had started my training, and I felt sick with regret and despair. This was an offence of the worst order. Miss Kay appropriately took me to task, but to her eternal credit she delivered the reprimand with understanding and kindness.

The patients at risk were closely monitored over the forthcoming days, and it was a great relief that none of them developed infections from my lack of observation, but it was an unforgivable mistake and a lesson which remained with me throughout my career.

It was very hard to be prepared for neurosurgical nursing. Many patients arrived on the ward seemingly well but with a distressing diagnosis and poor prognosis. Some recovered well after their surgery, but many went downhill and became very ill and subsequently died. Sister Cavell was remarkable, and the teamwork between the medical and nursing staff played a major role in looking after the patients under what were very difficult circumstances and with limited diagnostic equipment – scans were instruments of the future not available to us. We were rarely off duty before 9pm and it was often 9.30, although we were supposed to finish at 8pm. I couldn't remember when my feet had hurt so much, and I confided in my diary that I wished I could unscrew my legs.

On 3rd March, about a month after arriving at Hill End, I had a very pleasant respite from ward work. It was my day off, and I was sent a message from Sister to ask if I would like to take Lesley, an eight-month-old baby, up to Barts to be photographed. Well, how could I resist? The lovable, chubby infant with her big brown eyes was a great favourite with us all, and it was heartbreaking to know that her brain tumour was inoperable.

I put on my best worsted, pale blue suit under which I wore a cotton blouse with its fashionable Peter Pan collar. We went on our way by taxi without incident. Lesley, with her head swathed in bandages, was a model baby. She sat quietly on my knee as we viewed the countryside together. I "mooed" and "baaed" as

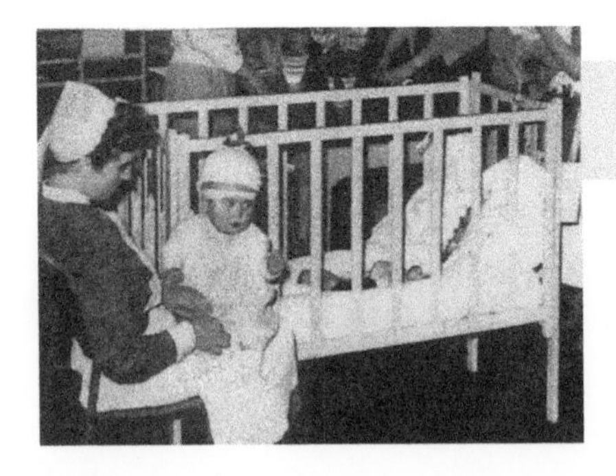

Lesley swathed in the head bandage.

appropriate when we passed fields of cows and sheep. Her podgy little hands and fingers touched my face (and my heart) as she gurgled happily before dropping off to sleep. I cuddled her with quiet self-satisfaction and confidence. Obviously, motherhood was a piece of cake.

I woke Lesley at the end of the journey; and as I lifted her up, she vomited all over the front of my suit. The sticky vomit made its way unforgivingly through to my fresh white blouse before reaching my underwear. Lesley just smiled, and I mopped both of us up as best I could. We sat in a room with other adults for some time, and I apologised to the assembled company for the dreadful state and foul smell of my outfit. Lesley clambered all over me and poked a finger in my eye, as eight-month-old babies do; she giggled and jiggled restlessly and pulled at her bandaged head, as we waited to be seen. Then, for no apparent reason, she howled and *howled*. I tried my best, without success, to look mature and in control. There was an empathetic silence in the waiting room before an Eastender, who was toothless and had lank mousey hair, spoke. 'This yer first babe, pet? I've got seven nippers at home and I can tell you, you ain't seen nothin' yet.'

To my shame I didn't reply. I *did* not and *would* not admit that I was not Lesley's mother. My maternal instinct came to the fore as the baby put her arms around my neck and wouldn't let go. I longed to say she was mine. The photographer's assistant appeared. 'Would Mummy like to bring the baby in now?' Well, at least I didn't have to tell a lie.

Fortunately, the photographic session went smoothly and Lesley settled. Peace reigned once more as we returned to Hill End, but I was exhausted and no longer felt that motherhood would be a walkover.

Nursing the adults on Cavell Ward wasn't a walkover either, but it was rewarding. Incontinence was a major problem for many of the patients, including Cyril, the Lancastrian, who had a pituitary tumour and who was a great favourite with us. Again and again, he would try and explain away his incontinence. 'My bed wet again? I dunno; that dog's been here again. I saw it come in, cock its leg and go out through the window. Look, there it is running across the grass!' We always agreed with him and laughed together.

Mr Creasey was another patient who knew his own mind and kept us in order.

'Mr Creasey, would you like to use a bottle?'

'When I want a Jimmy Riddle, Madam, I shall have a Jimmy Riddle. Until then, I shall not.'

This put paid to our question, although shortly after his tirade we would inevitably find a bed drenched in urine, but somehow it didn't matter, and he was washed and we changed his sheets yet again.

Mrs Simmons was not an incontinent patient but an inspirational one. When her head was shaved before her operation, there were no tears, just a thought for everyone else as she made the others waiting for their turn laugh as the shaving progressed. She kept a lock of her hair and put it carefully in a Swan Vestas matchbox and was the only patient I remember who asked to look in the mirror to see her baldness and did not even flinch at the sight.

During our mealtimes, we talked about our patients incessantly, and we never ceased to enjoy hearing stories from others about their wards, particularly about the conjoined twins,

Jeremy and Timothy Thackeray, who had recently been patients at Hill End.

There had been much interest and coverage from the national press about the Thackeray twins since their birth on 2nd May 1958. The babies were craniopagus twins, which meant they had fused skulls that only allowed them to lie end to end and they were unable to see each other. The twins were under the care of the eminent paediatrician Dr Alfred Franklin who was a colleague and close friend of Mr John O'Connell the neurosurgeon. After much discussion and preparation, it was decided to move the twins to Hill End for the neurosurgeon to carry out the first separation ever in England of this type of conjoined twins.

On the night of 22nd March 1959, the babies left Barts, not by ambulance, as would have been expected, but in an ordinary car to avoid the ever-watching press, who were on high alert to confirm the rumours of the imminent separation. The babies were "smuggled" out of the children's ward to the waiting vehicle, driven by none other than the eminent paediatrician himself. It was a hazardous journey to St Albans and not without incident; there was not only a pea soup smog in London but dense fog the rest of the way and the car plunged headlong into a ditch. The "driver", the babies and the two accompanying nursing Sisters, although somewhat shocked, were fortunately unhurt. The car was pulled to safety, and although it was a dramatic start to the twins' future, there was no panic and the journey continued.

In spite of the cloak and dagger operation, a newspaper reporter had managed to get wind of the impending separation, and on the night the twins arrived he was found prowling round the neurosurgical unit. The canny staff had foreseen this eventuality and had taken precautions to install the babies safely behind locked doors in a nearby anaesthetic room to spend their last night together as "one". According to the Night Sister,

Sybil Allen, the reporter was unknowingly standing just a few feet away from his sensational scoop and only realised he had missed his opportunity when the story broke twenty-four hours later.

The operation to separate the twins took place as planned on 23rd March by Mr O'Connell and his large and specialised team. John O'Connell was a devout Roman Catholic, and the moral dimensions of being the first to attempt the separation of craniopagus twins in England must have weighed heavily on him. The interminably long operation finally concluded successfully with both babies surviving.

The press invaded Hill End. Reporters entered the grounds without permission, and although they were refused entry to the wards, they relentlessly pursued individual staff and finally climbed up the outside walls to take photos through the ward windows. To them, of course, this was hot news; but to the medical and nursing staff, the priority was to look after the two little individuals. In those days, there were no hospital spokesmen, and John O'Connell encountered the full weight of Fleet Street's interest when it was, and should have been, his last concern.

Sadly, Jeremy never recovered his strength and he died seven months after the operation, but Timothy survived; and although he never recovered from a degree of brain damage, he was able to go home a year later to join his family in Manchester. John O'Connell, a quiet, modest and extremely conscientious man, rose to reluctant international fame almost overnight and went on to separate two more sets of conjoined twins.

*

To my surprise, I suddenly found I was enjoying the work and the ambience at Hill End. I *had* got used to it. Instead of having a lie in when I was off duty, I hired a bike and was joined one day by Anna and Priscilla, and we cycled into the glorious Hertfordshire countryside and ended up in St Albans having tea at a traditional tea shop where we ate Danish pastries and felt *normal*. On another day off, I went to see the film *Ben Hur* in London and drooled over Charlton Heston but arrived back to find myself locked out and had to climb through the open window, but even this was better than facing the porters at Barts. A friend and I occasionally thumbed a lift on an early morning flower lorry on its way from St Albans to Covent Garden, and I can't remember how many times I slept in an unsuspecting night nurse's bed, but I would always look forward to my return.

Still, my time at this run-down hospital was drawing to a close. We were very shortly to move the final wards, which had been at Hill End for so long, back to London. On 3rd April, the Dean of St Albans preached at a special Thanksgiving service, and it was very touching to hear of the good working relationship that had been in existence over many years between the two such very different hospitals.

Already the dormitory was beginning to empty. It was becoming increasingly eerie, and I had not heeded some of the advice given by my first friendly advisor. On the night of 14th April I woke to a muffled crackling coming from my wastepaper bin, which sounded suspiciously mouse-like. At 2.30am, I welcomed the hospital's black cat, which had wandered into my cubicle – I had high hopes of his mouse-catching capabilities, but it appeared he was unable to track down the rustling and he lost interest and went off disdainfully, possibly to find a hunting ground more to his liking. The rustling continued. At 3.30am, the cat reappeared but was once again disappointed. It was just beginning to get light at 5am when for a final time he returned and still he had no luck. It felt like a scene from a *Tom and Jerry* cartoon, and in common with the cartoon character, the mouse won hands down.

Two days later, there were only four of us left in the dormitory. The cockroaches, which we had kept at bay, now crept from under the floorboards and came out to play. On the night before we were due to abandon our sleeping quarters, Jo, one of my roommates, was getting undressed when a man appeared at the open window and peered in. After taking a good look, he lumbered on his way – it was very unsettling. We never found out whether the man was a peeping Tom or a psychiatric patient, but Jo slept on the floor in my cubicle for the night. It was a tight fit but worth it for peace of mind.

Cavell Ward was one of the last wards to move back to London, and the 18th April 1961 was our last full day at Hill End. The empty ward with its stripped beds and old wooden floorboards looked desolate and as though it was reluctant to let us go.

I travelled back by ambulance with Sister Cavell and two severely ill patients, one of which was the brave and still smiling Mrs Simmons, who had her lock of hair safely tucked away.

As a final goodbye, Sister told me she had been playing her latest record *Fings Ain't Wot They Used to Be* by Lionel Bart and sung by Max Bygraves. As we drove away for the last time, we agreed that nothing could ever replace the camaraderie and care carried out at dear old Hill End. She jumped into the ambulance clutching a vase of flowers. 'To make our new ward feel more homely,' she said.

Working at Hill End was an experience I would not have missed for the world. We had laughed. We had cried. We had worked under difficult conditions, but that had never compromised our care.

Infections were almost unheard of, but perhaps we will never know the reason why. I wondered whether this was to do with being in the country or whether it was because we never stopped cleaning. I felt bereft, but I had learnt a big lesson – the dilapidated state of the premises in which one worked counted for almost nothing; what really counted was the people who worked in them. I had more than "got used" to Hill End – I *loved* it.

Chapter Thirteen

WG Grace and the Blonde

Back to smoggy old London and the resulting smutty grey underwear. The new modern Elizabeth II Wing stood a little apart from the main hospital in an area of about half an acre, which had previously been occupied by bomb-damaged properties. The outside of the building was typical of architecture from the 1960s; it was visually unappealing and had an unattractive flat roof.

Although the neurosurgical ward at Hill End had been named Cavell in honour of the nurse heroine Edith Cavell (who was shot during the First World War by the Germans for assisting the escape of British soldiers), the new ward, would you believe, was named after a "mere" cricketer. I wondered who had been responsible for the decision – it must have been a man – and what relationship could this cricketer have had with the hospital?

The individual of note was William Gilbert Grace (known as WG), whom, at the time, I had never heard of but was considered "the greatest cricketer England had ever known". Grace, who was born in 1848, had been cricket-mad from a very young age, and by the time he was twenty, he was already becoming famous as a cricketer. This is not what his doctor father wished for him. Dr Grace Sr dearly wanted WG to follow in his medical footsteps. Due to his cricketing prowess, but not his academic ability, WG received overtures from both Oxford and Cambridge universities to study medicine, but his father insisted he enrol at the nearby Bristol Medical School. The young man continued to play cricket endlessly when he was a medical student, but it took him ten long years to qualify; and it was during his final two years, when the "mature" student was in London, that he was coached by Professor Howard Marsh from Barts and he at last managed to qualify at the age of thirty-one. He insisted that his success in his final exams was entirely due to intensive coaching from the Professor. When WG Grace died at the age of fifty-three, *The Times* paid tribute to *a cricket career that has not been equalled by any cricketer in the past and is not likely to be in the future*. Perhaps he was deserving of having a ward named after him, but I remember thinking it would have been more appropriate if we could have retained the name Cavell.

*

It was surprisingly heavy going on WG Grace Ward. The long Nightingale-style ward where Sister could keep an eye on all her patients had been replaced by small four-bedded wards, segregated for men and women, and one eight-bedded ward. The rules still applied, though, never to be forgotten – "wheels of the beds turned inwards, pillowcase openings away from the door". I had never questioned the latter rule and always assumed it was to provide a tidy ward, but apparently it had stemmed from Florence Nightingale during the Crimean War when she asserted that the only way to stop the sand blowing into the pillows from the harsh wind outside was to make sure the pillowcase openings faced away from the door.

A new break with tradition was the introduction of a Nurses' Station which was situated along a corridor; the value of this felt questionable as it alienated us from having close contact with the patients, and it meant our backs rather than our eyes faced the patients. A well-received innovation, though, was a Day Room for ambulant patients to give them a semblance of normality. As was customary, Sister had her own sitting room, furnished to her personal taste and into which she could retreat when she so wished.

I continued to be fifth nurse, and one of my daily duties was to collect the ward drugs from the dispensary in an enormous butcher's basket and, best of all, at the same time, to visit Helen, the Post Keeper. Helen knew everyone, and probably everyone's business as well, for it was she who sorted and manned all the incoming post for the nurses. Ever popular, she was always delighted when a nurse's pigeon hole was full of letters and equally sympathetic when it was empty. My task was to collect the letters for all the nurses on the ward. Letters were our lifeline. Access to the payphone – our only other means of communication with the outside world – always involved a long queue and the need to have a pocket full of small change. On returning to the ward, I distributed the post unobtrusively to the lucky individuals, who tucked their correspondence neatly under the bib of their aprons, relishing the feeling of anticipation.

I was in charge of two impressive sterilising rooms on the ward in which were large, unrecognisable boilers. These *obviously* required a degree in engineering to control, and it took me time to understand their complexity. This was nothing compared with problems of the autoclaves in the operating theatres of the new wing. One had exploded during a tense operating session and had caused the door to blow off and crash to the floor. According to the two nurses who were standing close by, the explosion nearly "snuffed the life" out of them; but they survived the ordeal, bravely pulled themselves together and brought the old fish kettles into immediate action to boil the instruments. Calm ensued, and the operation was barely interrupted.

One of the nurses involved in the autoclave explosion was a year ahead of me and was the aristocratic Priscilla d'Eresby Willoughby. This Priscilla (not to be confused with my close friend Priscilla) was always known as Prilli and was a descendant of Baron Willoughby d'Eresby who had been made a peer as far back as 1313. Her family had been very closely associated with St Bartholomew's Hospital and the City of London for over 300 years, and her grandmother's family on her father's side included physicians from Barts in the eighteenth century. Her grandfather, father and brother all trained at the hospital one generation after another; and her grandfather and father had both held the highly distinguished position of Medical Officer for the Port and City of London. Prilli was weaned on the history of Barts.

I first met her when we both represented the hospital at tennis. She was blonde, beautiful, tall, funny, fearless, friendly, outrageous and clever, and drove all the women in blue to distraction. She made it her business to know everyone, from the humble kitchen maid to the medical knights of the realm, and treated everyone the same. Her outgoing personality was like a magnet, and we all wanted to be counted as one of her best friends. Educated at an all-girls' boarding school convent, she had excelled at tennis, badminton, netball and ping pong, and played the organ and the piano with distinction.

Seemingly, she was also adept at singing Gregorian chants and had managed to pass a clutch of 'O' levels, including Latin. There was really no option as to what career she should pursue on leaving school. The God-given pathway had to be followed: nursing at Barts. Where else? But was she suited for such a serious vocational career?

The "breath of fresh air" arrived at Piggotts Manor for her preliminary training, where it never occurred to her that rules were made to be followed and her own particular brand of nursing was not quite the same as the hospital's. 'I received a shock at the end of PTS,' she once said to me, 'when the redoubtable Senior Tutor Miss Cape, recommended that I rethink my ideas of becoming a nurse and perhaps turn to the stage instead.'

Prilli set off immediately to London for an audience with Matron, where she managed to persuade the matriarch that she had already labelled her trunk for delivery to the Nurses' Home and that her parents were delighted that she had settled in so well. Miss Loveridge relented but placed the young free spirit on the professorial unit under Sister Stanmore, who didn't stand any nonsense from anyone, whoever they were, and the Sister immediately delegated second-year nurse Joan Capps, the daughter of the ENT surgeon Mr Freddie Capps, to "keep a watchful eye" on the new pro.

Things didn't go too well. After three months on the ward there were a number of domestic incidents that were obviously going to count against Prilli. 'There was the unfortunate day,' she recalled, 'when I had placed boiled eggs in the oven to keep them warm and they came out as hard as bullets, and another when I failed to get Lord Ismay's poached egg to poach even though Sister had shown me how to do it the day before. Perhaps worst of all, though, was my skate down the ward in a Ronuk polish tin when I ended up under a bed surrounded by gallipots and broken thermometers – just at the arrival of the professorial ward round.'

These events did not bode well for Prilli's upcoming election three days later. On the evening before the important day of judgement, fate interceded when, on her way to a party, she re-enacted her Ronuk polish debacle to her friends and genuinely slipped and hurt her arm. Nevertheless, never one to miss a jolly, off she went. It was after midnight when the revellers returned and, along with the others, Prilli, nursing her sore arm, was fed through the window into the Path Lab. As they made their way across the Square towards the Nurses' Home, they congratulated themselves on escaping the attention of the Night Porter, but then unexpectedly they bumped into Dr Coulson – the doctor responsible for all the nurses' health.

'Nurse Willoughby,' he said, 'you look a bit peaky,' and asking no further questions, he escorted her into the loving arms of Ormi in the Nurses' Sickrooms in the middle of the night. It transpired that Prilli had broken her wrist and had snapped the head off her radius. 'I missed the Elections,' she said, 'had my arm fixed, spent three weeks on sick leave, and everyone conveniently seemed to forget that I had never officially passed or indeed failed the all-important test.'

Prilli was a great storyteller, and we all enjoyed hearing of her experience the first time she attended Matron's Ball at the Grosvenor House Hotel in 1959. 'I was getting a bit desperate,' she recounted, 'about ever finding a suitable date for the evening, when Lily Heed, one of my much-loved patients, who was a brittle diabetic, begged me to ask *her* young doctor. At that very moment, the young "doctor" was struggling to elicit Lily's sugar status by boiling her urine in the sluice, which was made more difficult because the poor lad was colour-blind and couldn't tell orange from blue.'

Prilli did as her patient bid and pursued the medical student into the privacy of the sluice. He was amazed at the invitation to a free dinner and dance at such a splendid venue and instantly accepted.

'The evening almost faltered from the start,' she said, 'as one of my "so-called" friends, having been to Moss Bros earlier in the day to collect our chosen hired gear, fell asleep on the bus on the way back to the hospital and woke up at Gamages bus stop in Ludgate Circus. She was in such a hurry she left my dress behind. Unsuspectingly, I came off duty with my hair in rollers under my cap, clutching a fur tippet given to me with much ceremony by Lily, along with a bottle of Lily of the Valley from the rest of the patients to dab behind my ears for full effect. I was ready to slide into my dress, but there was nothing to slide into.'

A deputation of other Grosvenor attendees arrived at Prilli's room to report the catastrophic incident, and there was a crisis meeting. It turned out that one of the girls had a spare ensemble, which she kindly offered to lend to the tall and lithe Prilli – a moss green taffeta strapless dress that had been designed especially for her small stature and forty-inch bust.

'In my borrowed green ballgown, I duly danced the night away, accompanied by my chosen student who thought I was wearing khaki, as he tried his very best to ignore the fact that the dress revealingly separated from me every time we jived.'

Prilli continued her relationship with her colour-blind student, John Stevens, for a protracted five and a half years during which, as an impecunious medical student, his idea of courtship included classy invitations to dinner and the theatre – the dinner was a split sausage, egg and chips at Pete's, followed by two free nurses' tickets to whatever was showing at the time. She and her

In her borrowed ballgown, Prilli danced the night away.

beau finally became engaged on View Day in 1964, and Prilli, at last, finally married her Mr Right at St Bartholomew the Great the same year with City ambulances ringing their bells with gusto and joy and with their mutual diabetic patient a guest of honour.

The "possibly/probably failed" probationer remained at the hospital for thirteen years, continuing to spread joy and provoke disapproval in all directions. She moved up the hierarchy and finally achieved her greatest prize of all and went into "blue" and was later to become world-famous in pioneering stoma therapy. What a turn-up for the books.

*

View Day took place shortly after my return to London from Hill End and was always a very special occasion. It was steeped in tradition, having been first held in 1551 and had never been cancelled, despite two world wars. The custom originated from the Easter services which were held in nearby Spitalfields and were designed to attract attention to the London hospitals. Apparently, patients were paraded through

View Day was a very smart affair.

the streets of London to the Easter services so they could be seen by the public, who naturally felt compassion for the patients' plight and made donations towards their care. However, by 1551, the custom of showing patients to the public was discontinued, and instead the governors, physicians and surgeons of the hospital took their place and View Day was born. In 1824, the date of the event was changed from Easter to May as the doctors declared it "extremely desirable" that View Day should be held "at a less inclement season". The second Wednesday in May was selected, and View Day has been held on that day ever since.

The sixteenth-century View Day inspections were chiefly concerned with arranging repairs and new leases for the many countryside properties owned by the hospital; but by the eighteenth century, the focus of View Day shifted back to the patient, and the governors invited the general public to visit the wards and see the patients and awarded prizes to the most attractive wards for their floral decorations.

There were no prizes for the floral decorations in 1961, but the Square became a riot of colour with an abundance of scarlet geraniums adorning all the ground-level window boxes, contrasting with the newly painted dark green roofs of the four shelters. Even the surrounding lamps were rendered spotless, apparently with the aid of bladder syringes filled with detergent. The fountain was a picture as the water cascaded merrily into the pool below. The magnificent plane trees were at their best as they showed off their camouflaged mixture of grey, olive and green-patterned bark, together with their spring leaves.

The Sisters rose very early on Wednesday 10th May to go to Covent Garden to choose flowers for their wards, after which they returned to arrange their own displays. Each ward chose a particular variety of flower for its emblem as well as appropriately coloured carnations for the medical staff's buttonholes of their morning dress. I was surprised to hear that green carnations were

The Beadle led the procession.

even available to coordinate with the "Green" firm.

During my lunch break, I changed my uniform in readiness for the afternoon inspection. As usual, I panicked about my millinery expertise until I was rescued by Jane, who, with her usual efficiency and artistry, pleated a beautiful fan-tailed showpiece, and I was ready to greet my visiting parents before the ceremony started. My mother, in common with all the women guests, was wearing a pretty, fashionable hat and looked very smart.

At 2pm, the Beadle, holding his staff aloft, accompanied Matron, the Steward and the Clerk to the governors as well as Sir George Aylwen, who was the Treasurer and the Chairman of the Board of Governors. They processed round the hospital visiting each immaculate ward whilst we nurses, in order of seniority, stood to attention with our hands behind our backs as each patient's name was read out by the Steward and they were asked if they had any cause for complaint. As if they dared? Although one lively Wag couldn't resist answering "Long live Guys!"

The procession was completed by honouring the memory of Rahere, the founder of the hospital, by the laying of a single rose at the foot of his tomb in the church of St Bartholomew the Great by a member of the nursing staff.

After the formalities were complete, the hospital was open to the public, which naturally included our parents. All the ward Sisters offered a splendid tea, but Heath Harrison Ward

Every in-patient in the hospital had their name read out by the Steward.

was the highest on the list to visit. Sister, whose parents were French, had impeccable taste, and she always placed her "once a year" magnificent highly polished silver tray on her desk to provide a frontispiece for the celebration, and on it sat a fine bone china tea set. Lawrence Ward was another popular venue. Sister, one of the larger members of the fraternity, was renowned for her famous homemade scones. It was well known that one of her eccentricities was her habit of appearing on her ward at 2am via the fire escape, which connected the Nurses' Home to her ward, to bake scones in readiness for Sir James Patterson Ross and his team after his ward round the following morning.

The sun always seemed to shine on View Day, and we were proud to belong to such a famous institution, and my parents were suitably impressed.

Today, the role of the governors on View Day has been superseded by the Lord Mayor of London and the Livery Companies; and whilst there is a grand procession to the church service in the Church of St Bartholomew the Great, the viewing of patients and the wards is no longer considered appropriate, and sadly, reunions from past medical and nursing staff have diminished.

*

After the excitement of View Day, everything felt a bit flat.

However, some of us had an important event to look forward to as Carol – one of our original set at PTS – was getting married in a matter of days. It seemed a long time since the mad cap girl had driven into Piggotts Manor on her spanking new Lambretta with Jackie. The nuptials, of course, necessitated the buying of a new outfit. My ensemble consisted of a full-skirted dress with black and white stripes, sprinkled with rosebuds. The hat (if you can call it that) was a fashionable bit of frippery made of black net with an artificial pink rose perched on top.

At last, Saturday 13th May arrived. A day fit for a beautiful bride. The ceremony took place in St Bartholomew the Great, and Carol, in her white fitted satin dress, was the envy of us all. The patients from the new Queen Elizabeth Block looked on from above, clapping and cheering – everything seemed to bode well for the couple's future, but unfortunately the marriage lasted only a short time, and Carol came back to see us a few months after her wedding saying she already regretted that she had not finished her training.

On a much happier note was the burgeoning romance between none other than Sister WG Grace and her Registrar Mr Hannigan. Rumour had it that Mr O'Connell, the neurosurgeon, had already had his suspicions that love was in the air. Apparently, he asked them both to dinner during which, as was his normal practice, he pressed the bell by his knee to summon his housekeeper to bring in the second course. There was a sudden shriek from Sister who had felt the movement next to her. 'Don't worry, Sister,' said the great man, 'it's only me, not Hannigan this time!' It was good to hear that my favourite Sister met her future husband, who later became a neurosurgeon, doing the work to which they were both dedicated, and three years later they were married.

My own relationships with the opposite sex were fairly low key during this period. There were several gauche medical students who invited me out for a cheap and cheerful cup of coffee, but when an upright and charming houseman, with the look of a military man, called David, wrote a fairly formal letter asking me out to dinner, how could I possibly refuse? I was always hungry and I couldn't resist the idea of a proper meal. The dinner, at the Chinese Bowl in South Kensington, was excellent and included sweet and sour pork, spring rolls, dumplings and chow mein. The best bit of all, though, was sailing through the gates at 11.45pm in the handsome young man's open-topped, racing green MG and giving a stately wave to the porters as I progressed through the Square without even having to show them my late pass.

*

During my time on WG Grace, our set celebrated our second anniversary. Two years completed, I still loved nursing and had managed not to have a day off sick. Life was good, but as usual it was hard not to worry about the patients. Dear Mrs Simmons had died, she who had so carefully saved her lock of hair. It hit me particularly hard as she had seemed so fit and well when she was admitted, and then she died because of the operation.

Nursing very sick children whose life expectancy was short was also heart-rending. There was seven-year-old Julia who had a brain tumour and was now suffering from bulbar paralysis and was not only blind but after every meal, food came down her nose. Still, she never stopped talking and was forever cheerful. In contrast, there was "black as your hat" Pauline, aged five, who had arrived straight from Jamaica and refused to utter a word to anyone.

'Can you get Pauline to say something? *Anything*,' I remember pleading with Julia. I guided her to Pauline's bed.

'Hello, Pauline. My name is Julia. Are you there? I'm blind so I can't see you.'

Silence from the bed.

'Pauline, I've got a present for you.'

A smile spread over the silent child's face as she reached out to take a bar of chocolate from Julia's sticky hand.

'Well, you might say thank you,' said the freckle-faced Julia. 'Remember, I can't *see* you but I can *hear* you.'

There was a little whisper of thanks. Julia was all smiles and put her thumbs up. She had succeeded where we had failed.

From then on, we couldn't stop Pauline talking, and she insisted on treating her own pressure areas. Julia was never sorry for herself and loved everyone as we loved her. The two little girls became the best of friends, but sadly Julia died within a few weeks and I never knew what happened to Pauline after she left us to go back home to Jamaica.

My time on WG Grace was drawing to a close, and I wrote in my diary that along with Cavell Ward at Hill End, it had been my favourite ward. Now, my day of doom was fast approaching – I was about to go on the most dreaded ward in the hospital.

Chapter Fourteen

Only a Smidgen of Milk and Honey

She looked me up and down through her thick lensed spectacles and then asked me to turn round. 'Nurse,' she said, 'you have a hole in the back of your stocking and I see that the top pocket in your uniform dress is stained with bright blue ink. I do not wish to have you working on my ward looking so disreputable. Please return to your room at once, and do not come back until this situation has been rectified.'

The stocking with its barely visible hole was now destined for the rubbish heap, and the ink on my dress was from my fountain pen which had leaked and was never to be removed. How *could* she? What a start. This did not augur well.

Sandhurst Ward was as bad as I had been told. There were wonderful patients, a lovely ward maid and great camaraderie with all the other suffering students, but Sister was truly awful.

I quickly realised that on this highly personal gynaecological ward, where we were dealing with diseases specific to the female reproductive system, we not only had to learn new techniques, but we also needed to develop special intuition and insight when dealing with illnesses of such an intimate nature. There was no doubt that the patients tended to be emotional, and there were many tearful outbursts, but what was overwhelmingly obvious was the support they gave to each other. All of them needed not only the skill of the doctor but also reassurance and kindness, as well as technical excellence, from their nurses.

The morale on Sandhurst Ward was low. This was in direct contrast to the other gynaecological ward where the Sister, although somewhat eccentric, was a delight. It was on her ward where she wouldn't allow her nurses to put red and white flowers together in a vase as this was considered to be bad luck, or to use chicken wire to keep the flowers upright in a vase because, she said, 'You wouldn't like *your* bottoms pushed through chicken wire.'

Time on Sandhurst felt endless. The atmosphere was tense. The short-sighted Sister was probably in her late forties, and all six foot of her towered above us. I spent the whole day on avoidance tactics. I wasn't the only one. I could see there was a great teamwork approach with only one mission in mind. *To keep out of Sister's way.* It was to our advantage that the ward layout was different from the general wards, and when we were in the sluice or the kitchen, we could spy the bane of our lives through the window as she sat primly at her desk.

There were no gynaecological operations on my first day, and apart from carrying out routine dressings and vaginal douches, we were not busy. We hid among the ever-shining monometal bedpans in the sluice and made ready to move as soon as Sister approached when we were alerted by the nurse on watch. Down we all went on the *other* side of the ward from the one chosen by Sister, busying ourselves by unnecessarily tidying an immaculate bed here and there. This happened time and again, and all four of us underemployed nurses made our way into the ward kitchen, where again a nurse was put on guard and the same process was repeated. I soon learnt that another way to avoid the wrath of Sister was to be seen cleaning and tidying cupboards. Some were scrubbed several times a day.

We were all required to work on a gynaecological ward to satisfy the curriculum, which is probably why we were greatly overstaffed during the day. In 1961, there were 683 nurses at the hospital, of whom two-thirds were students in training and seventy-four were Sisters. By the late 1960s, there were 838 nursing staff, and for the first time in history the hospital could claim to employ one nurse for every bed; but even in 1961, there were plenty of student nurses to go round.

The Sisters, like their predecessors, had a working day whose hours were fixed by custom rather than written contract. They could use their discretion to stop work when they felt they could safely do so, but they often worked continuously from 8am until 8.30pm.

Sister Sandhurst was rarely away from her ward and obviously had a high sense of responsibility. To give her credit, she was always charming to those under her care, but such niceties did not seem to stretch to her workforce. Mealtimes, which she never missed, were the worst, and we all tried to avoid being her assistant as she sallied forth with the gleaming pudding trolley, always with its creamy rice pudding.

She was known for her catchphrase as she served out the pudding to the patients. 'Shug shug on your pud pud?' she would enquire sweetly. In the next breath, she would turn to the shaking nurse whose trembling hands were spilling the sugar all over the serving trolley. 'You silly, incompetent child; mop up the mess immediately.'

Sister Sandhurst was very religious and was the church warden of our little church, but we could never fathom out why she was so holy one minute and so disagreeable the next. Prayers were always said on the ward before Sister went off duty; and on that first day, as I dutifully bowed my head in prayer, I thanked God that I had managed to reach the end of my first day relatively unscathed.

Day two was equally nerve-racking, and I longed to be anywhere but Sandhurst Ward. To Sister's wrath, I managed to flood the polished wooden oak floor as I attempted to carry out my very first vaginal douche. Fortunately, Mrs O'Brien, the delightful Australian patient, thought the whole charade very amusing, and it was she who understood my awkwardness and made up for Sister's wrath. I found that however inadequate the undertaking of a task, the patients were always on our side.

Operation Day arrived and the atmosphere could have been cut with a knife. There had to be complete silence throughout the ward once the pre-medications had been given prior to the patients being wheeled on a trolley down to the operating theatre. Even talking to a patient was considered by Sister as "doing nothing", whereas we felt that a word of encouragement for those awaiting surgery could only be a good thing.

By the end of the day, I was so fraught that Priscilla and I pilfered her piggy bank, counted out twenty sixpences (the equivalent of 50p), and we went to see the smash hit musical *My Fair Lady* starring Julie Andrews and Rex Harrison. It was well worth it.

*

On Saturday, 27 May, Beth returned from her TB convalescence looking a picture of health. She was about to start on the Eye Ward, which, according to Matron, was to "break her in gently". It was so good to have her back and, in true Beth fashion, she took it in her stride and didn't even seem to mind she had dropped two sets.

No sooner had Beth come back, than I was put on internal night duty on Sandhurst and had to work twelve nights on the trot: the first six nights as a junior and the following six as the senior. The very thought of being in charge was daunting enough, but even worse was the thought of having to give Sister the night report. I was a nervous wreck on my first night of seniority and was rescued only by Beth and Priscilla, who visited me late at night dressed in mufti. They had dined out and had smuggled in a "doggy bag" full of fried bread, cheese and ham and an egg – all for three shillings and sixpence. Delicious.

*

Sandhurst wasn't all about dodging Sister, and whilst I was on night duty, Her Majesty the Queen was due to open the hospital's new Queen Elizabeth II block, and preparations were well underway. Many monarchs had had close connections with the hospital over the centuries, and two of our doctors, one a surgeon and the other a physician, were by appointment to Her Majesty.

Sir James Patterson Ross was one of these exalted beings. Over the years, he had risen to an eminent position in the medical profession, and in 1949 he had looked after King George VI when the monarch developed serious blood supply problems in one of his legs. Surgeon Ross, along with Sir James Learmouth, was called upon to undertake a lumbar sympathectomy to relieve the problem; and for his time, trouble and expertise, he was created KCVO whilst the King was still in bed recuperating – surely the only time a subject has been dubbed by a monarch in pyjamas?

On the Queen's accession in 1952, Sir James was appointed Surgeon to Her Majesty; and in 1960, he was made a baronet. It was known, and all of us had seen first-hand, that our Sir

James was not only an excellent communicator, clinician and administrator but was also recognised for his sound judgement and his sympathetic understanding of his patients. Sir Winston Churchill was one such patient, and Sir James assisted Sir Thomas Dunhill in repairing the great man's very large inguinal hernia just after the end of the Second World War, which, to everyone's satisfaction, but particularly that of the patient, was carried out not in a hospital but on a kitchen table in a private home.

Sir Ronald Bodley Scott was the other "anointed" being. Sir Ronald was always a source of interest to those of us who were students. This was not, I have to admit, entirely due to his eminence, which was without question – he was a world authority on leukaemia and lymphoma – but because he was easily recognisable due to his wearing of the newly introduced "half-moon spectacles" which were always perched on the end of his nose. He was an expert with the written word and edited *Price's Textbook of the Practice of Medicine*, but perhaps even more important was that he earned the love and loyalty of all those who worked for him. He had no sons of his own, only daughters, and he treated his young male students almost as adopted sons. In 1949, he was appointed Physician to the Household of King George VI and in 1952 became Physician to the Queen and later received a knighthood which was advanced to a GCVO.

Dawn was already breaking at 4.50am on Tuesday, 30th May, 1961, the day of the Queen's visit; and when I looked out of the window of Sandhurst Ward onto the deserted Square, the cascade of the fountain appeared to be falling serenely. The sky was cloudless with just a hint of the pink sunrise about to touch the tops of the City of London's buildings, and the plane trees were nearly at their magnificent best with their burgeoning ball-shaped white flowers contrasting with the vibrant geraniums already in place. It was surely going to be a day fit for a Queen, I wished she could have seen the Square as I saw it then – tranquil and undisturbed.

I was working my fifth night and had seven more to go, but I wasn't going to miss the afternoon's royal occasion. I slept fitfully until lunchtime and then, bleary-eyed, joined my friends in the Nurses' Dining Room. No mufti today, just exquisitely pleated caps and freshly laundered uniform.

We made our way to the Square amid a throng of nurses all jockeying for a good viewing position. A number of patients, some in their beds and others in wheelchairs, were happily settled as they also waited to catch a glimpse of the Queen. The balconies overlooking the Square were full to capacity, and we could see faces peering over window ledges and window boxes.

We were ready, as were our very best – including Matron and her Deputies and all the Sisters who were all on show for the special occasion – and we were more than ready to provide support.

At 2.30pm sharp, an immaculate black Rolls Royce with its Royal Standard fluttering sedately from the roof drove smoothly and slowly under the archway and into the Square. The normally elusive grey and white hospital cat made a surprise guest appearance and had the audacity to stop right in

The hospital's cat seemed relaxed about the Queen's visit.

front of Her Majesty's limousine and only just managed to avoid being run over. A lucky escape – I wondered if he had come to "Look at the Queen" as in the children's famous nursery rhyme.

We applauded as the Queen stepped gracefully out of her car, and I caught a glimpse of her summery primrose and white printed silk dress which was covered by a matching coat. Her hat was petal-like and close-fitting, which I thought had the look of a swimming cap, but was nevertheless rather pretty. She was greeted by her uncle, the Duke of Gloucester, who was president of the hospital, and Mr Enoch Powell Minister of Health and, of course, Matron.

Naturally, the welcoming party included the hospital's royal doctors, Sir James Patterson Ross and Sir Ronald Bodley Scott, both resplendent in their gowns. Within no time at all, though, Her Majesty was whisked away to perform her royal duties and the Square returned to its workaday normal, and I went back to a sleepless afternoon in bed.

The Queen, however, had better things to do, and after receiving a bouquet to match her outfit she met the curtseying senior nursing staff, all of whom, especially Belinda the Operating Theatre Superintendent, performed to perfection. The invited dignitaries were already assembled in the Great Hall in anticipation of Her Majesty's speech, which by all accounts didn't disappoint. Her closing

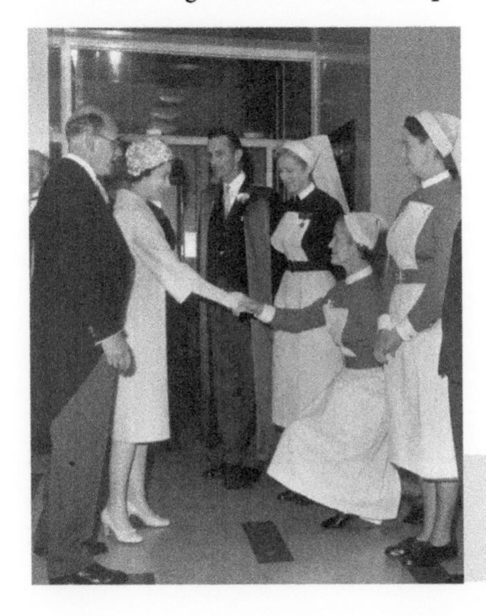

Gracious curtseys from the Sisters as they greeted Her Majesty.

words were highly appropriate for the occasion:

'Whatever success the future may bring, the traditions of Saint Bartholomew's, which reach back to the year 1123, will be carried on, as they are today, in the interests of your patients, in the teaching of your students and in the continuation of research.'

Sir George Aylwen, the Treasurer and Chairman of the Board of Governors, and so, in effect, our boss, responded and paid a heartfelt compliment to his doctors and nurses:

'Your Majesty, you have been graciously pleased to receive a bouquet. I will presume to offer you a simple nosegay, a mystical nosegay, made up of those flowers which bloom so abundantly in the wards and operating theatres, indeed in all parts of this great and ancient hospital where nurses, surgeons and physicians do foregather – the flowers of Self-Sacrifice, Patience, Tolerance, Courage, Kindness and Understanding. The flowers are bound together with that never-failing perennial – Service.'

What a tribute to his multidisciplinary team at St Bartholomew's.

The Queen officially opened the Queen Elizabeth II Surgical Block and the "up-to-the-minute" radiotherapy department before moving on to Gloucester House, the new Nurses' Home, where the modern training department for nurses was housed. As she watched demonstrations of nursing procedures, she was heard to remark that she thought that practical teaching was of the utmost importance. Next, Her Majesty took tea with the governors and their wives before she was whisked away to attend yet another important function.

*

When we were working on Sandhurst Ward, time often hung heavily on night duty, but when Nurse Horan joined me as my Night Junior, things looked up when we became "partners in crime". Sue Horan was none other than the daughter of a bishop. Her parentage, however, made absolutely no difference to the way she behaved, and together we delighted in devising pranks, one of which we were quite proud. It was unusually hot one night and we had opened the windows overlooking the Square. Canoodling couples were happily walking below on their way to the Nurses' Home. They were naturally oblivious to everything and everybody but themselves. It was too good an opportunity to miss.

'What shall we do?' said the bishop's daughter.

'Water, feathers, bandages and paper clips should do the trick,' I replied, trying to suppress my laughter.

We collected a jugful of water, six tumblers, a feather pillow, bandages and paper clips and set about disturbing the romantic couples. Paper clips were fastened to long lengths of crepe bandage, the glass tumblers were filled with water and the pillow containing the feathers was slit open. We were set to go.

A couple, hand in hand, drifted by and halted under the window for a romantic moment during which we dropped handfuls of feathers from above; these floated downwards like entirely improbable snowflakes. The lovers didn't even notice.

The next cuddling couple were treated to what we felt was our pièce de résistance. The unfurled bandages, weighted by the attached paper clips, were dangled from above and allowed to dance around the pair's embracing faces as they stood below. When, inevitably, they looked up, we emptied the tumblers of water onto their upturned faces. Whereupon, giggling uncontrollably, we ducked out of sight, but we could hear the unperturbed laughter below.

'Thanks, girls,' said a male voice as he acknowledged the gift from the perpetrators on high. 'We needed cooling off in more ways than one.'

We had played a childish prank, but we had had to do *something* to take our minds off the excessive heat. Of course,

I was far from innocent, but the bishop's daughter – *she* should have known better.

My mind needed taking off the excessive heat, but the escapade did not take my mind off romance. It must have been in the air. On 17th June, when I was at home after the debilitating non-stop twelve nights, I unexpectedly received a telephone call.

'Are you free to play tennis? I'm short of a fourth.' It was David, an old acquaintance and the brother of Clive who had been my tennis partner in my youth. Clive, when he was thirteen, had declared that when he was old enough, he would marry me. This momentous and extraordinary declamation took place as we sat together on a double-decker bus on our way to Birmingham to play in a tennis tournament when the youngster suddenly turned to me and said, 'I bet you a pound I'll marry you.'

I recall feeling very pleased at the thought – he was such a talented tennis player. He was also what I imagined my "Laurie" of *Little Women* would have looked like, with his dark curly hair and equable temperament; so it seemed a good match.

This childhood episode had nothing to do with his brother David, who was his elder by four years, and *I* had nothing better to do when David telephoned. The twenty-five-year-old arrived to pick me up for the tennis date with his whites and racquet neatly packed away in his sports bag. He had come straight from work and was dressed in a charcoal grey suit, a white shirt with a detachable stiff collar (à la Mr Medcalf, the diabetes sufferer on Rahere Ward) and was wearing an old school tie. He was not scruffy, he was not wearing a white coat and he certainly didn't have a stethoscope around his neck. All was not lost, though – it was worth a go.

The game didn't start too well when I saw David had forgotten to do up his fly buttons on his tennis shorts and it was putting me off my game. As we changed sides of the tennis court I whispered, 'David, your flies are undone.'

'Sorry. What did you say?'

'Your flies are undone.' I didn't know this young man very well, and the tennis court was a very different environment from the hospital situation where I was used to seeing men in various stages of undress.

'*Your fly buttons are not done up!*' I whispered urgently.

He turned his back on me to rectify the problem, and we continued the rather erratic game of doubles, after which we agreed to meet the next evening and subsequently the next... and the next. These rendezvous were, of course, just for a game of tennis, you understand. However, on the second evening when he took me home, to my surprise, and without permission, he suddenly kissed me.

Three days later, on Tuesday, 20th June, 1961, I knew I was in love. My parents knew it, too. My father reported excitedly to my mother that he had caught sight of me putting mascara on my eyelashes – an unheard-of exercise.

I dreaded the thought of going back to work for another twelve nights to face Sister and her never-ending criticism and continual ill humour, and the thought of leaving David was almost unbearable. On my return to the hospital, I found that my friends had put a single pink rose bud in a brandy glass and a lovely vase of flowers in my room with a note expressing their sympathy for my return to the dreaded ward. What they didn't know was that as well as condolences, there was cause for celebration.

The next day, I found a note on my door from Anna:

If you go to my room pronto you will find something to your advantage on my bed.

Five, heavily starched, white belts were lying neatly across Anna's bed. Mine were too large; it would appear they had been made for a plump individual, and I had to make them fit my slender waist. I used the pointed end of my scissors as a hole puncher and inserted the studs. Once tightly belted, I couldn't resist a quick twirl in front of the mirror. I could be identified as a third-year nurse at last.

Carrying out the duties of a junior for the next six nights meant it was back to making and serving the night drinks, washing up, rolling sanitary towels and polishing the bedpans. This didn't go down too well now I was in my white belt and my night senior, confusingly, was only a mere second-year nurse.

Considering it was only early summer, the weather continued to be unbelievably hot. Each day, in the late afternoon, I left a restless bed and walked to the Embankment in search of a breeze and watched the large and small boats and ships go by on the Thames. At night, I was grateful for the lightweight cotton nightdress sent to me by my parents.

On another baking hot day, I didn't go to bed at all; instead, I went with David to Wimbledon who had two prized Centre Court tickets for the Tennis Championships. I was able to tell him that it was largely due to a Barts doctor that the tennis championships at Wimbledon ever came to being in the first place. Apparently, a doctor called Henry "Cavendish" Jones gave up medicine to become a sports journalist and became a committee member of the All England Croquet Club and was successful in introducing tennis at the club, which was renamed the All England Lawn Tennis Club. However, in 1877, the club was in financial trouble and there was no money to pay for the repair of a broken pony roller which had been used to roll the grass tennis courts. Henry and his friends hit on the idea of holding a Gentlemen's Singles Tennis Tournament to raise funds for its repair. This insignificant, but successful, event, with just twenty-two competitors, was the precursor of the now world-famous Wimbledon Championships, and here we were – all ready to watch Rod Laver in action.

Most of the spectators in 1961 were smartly dressed, with the gentlemen in suits and ties and the ladies wearing elegant frocks and large, wide-brimmed hats which were secured with hat pins. I went hatless, ever mindful of the people sitting behind me who wanted, as I did, to follow the game uninterrupted without the need to hat-dodge.

The Centre Court was in mint condition, and Laver, who went on to win the Men's Singles Championship, played a magnificent match with his trusty wooden Dunlop Maxply racquet. The ball boys from the local Dr Barnardo's Home looked very smart in their purple and dark green uniforms; and the waitresses, in their traditional black skirts and white blouses, served strawberries and cream to all and sundry. We had a very good day, and I even managed to keep awake before going straight from the tennis on to ten more nights on duty.

I was in love. There was no doubt about it, but I was surprised by my certainty. I had known David from a distance as Clive's much older brother when I used to stay at his parents' house, but he had always seemed to be in his room studying. I had remembered he was a shy, very good-looking six-footer who was an avid sports player, keen skier and academically very bright, but these qualities didn't entirely explain why I fell in love with him. But I knew, I very much knew, that fundamentally, even after a few short days, I was in for the "long haul", even if I was doomed to discuss sport for evermore.

Back at the hospital I had now reverted to the position of senior nurse, termed the "Night Staff" and was therefore in charge of Sandhurst Ward at night. This meant I had to give the report to Sister each morning. I was always in trouble for one thing or another; but one morning, for once, Sister didn't utter a word. Was I giving such a good report she had nothing to say? Sadly, no. She was totally engrossed in her daily task of completing beautiful graphs with perfectly formed dots joined by straight ruled lines denoting all the patients' temperatures over the previous twenty-four hours. This task appeared of greater importance than my pearls of wisdom.

Shortly after I had finished my spell of night duty, I was due to change wards. What a blessed relief. I was summoned to see the ever-popular Assistant Matron, Miss Harper. 'Good Morning, Nurse Tisdale. I see you are working on Sandhurst Ward and at the end of the month you are due to go on holiday. Are you planning to go somewhere exciting?' This seemed a fairly unusual question and was not one that the office matrons had asked of me previously.

'Yes, Miss Harper. I will be spending a week of it with Nurse Robbins (Meg) in St Leonards-on-Sea at a Pathfinder Camp where we will be cooking for about 200 disadvantaged city children.'

She looked down at her chart, with a slight frown on her face, perhaps hoping I had been going to say I was off to the South of France to laze on a sunny Mediterranean beach.

'Well, it looks as though we will be short of nursing staff on Sandhurst Ward until the end of the month, and I would like you to remain there until you go away.'

My face must have been a picture. She took one look at my horrified expression and understood. 'Never mind, dear,' she said, 'during the rest of your time on the ward, just think of the delicious food you will be cooking for the dear little children.'

Miss Harper knew how much we all disliked working on Sandhurst and was sympathetic, but she had to be loyal to her colleagues, and there was little she could say other than to empathise.

The very thought of remaining on Sandhurst, if only for several very long weeks, was loathsome. However, at least I could look forward to David's visit, and we went to see *Ross* at the Haymarket Theatre followed by dinner at Luba's Bistro, and enjoyed the atmosphere of the restaurant with its cheery chef/proprietor and his gingham red-checked table cloths and dripping candles in Chianti bottles. Towards the end of the evening, we went for coffee at the Sou-Sol café in Wigmore Street, but the pleasure was outweighed by the pain of having to say our farewells through the bars of the locked Henry VIII Gate.

On Friday 21st July, I went home for my day off and wanting to impress David with my culinary prowess, I proudly cooked him spaghetti bolognese and was pleased when he accepted the offer of a second helping. It wasn't until much later that I learnt that he had never been able to bear the sliminess of any sort of pasta; and since his gallant behaviour on that occasion, no spaghetti has ever again passed his lips.

After supper, the evening took on a different note when we went for a drive in David's rather boring, insipid-looking, pale grey Mini. He stopped the car on a deserted countryside road a short distance from my home and turned off the ignition. Without preamble, and entirely unlike his usual, measured self, he suddenly said, 'Will you marry me? I love you and I would like you to be the mother of my children.'

'Yes, of course,' I replied, entirely *in* character and without a moment's hesitation. And that was that, after only a month's sporadic courtship. I'm sure my parents thought I was destined to wed a dedicated doctor and not a besuited "boring" chartered accountant, but I knew a good man when I saw one and was without any doubts. So, I supposed I was now unofficially engaged. Keeping the news to myself was going to be agonisingly difficult; still, there was nothing for it; it was time to get back to night duty and Sister – thank goodness for the patients.

My last few days on Sandhurst Ward were just about bearable. Before I took my leave, Sister even asked me where I was going to for my holiday. Although she stopped short of wishing me a good time, it was a great improvement. I was off – St Leonards and the cooking pots were simmering.

Chapter Fifteen

Skins, Nits and the Samaritans

The Pathfinder children evidently enjoyed our cooking judging by how much they ate; the preparation of 200 meals three times a day had been quite a challenge, and the peeling of the potatoes had felt like a never-ending marathon. My second week at home was more restful, and I decided it was time I learnt how to drive a car. It was a simple exercise in the 1960s – I received a couple of "romantic" driving lessons from David, had one charming and forgiving examiner, and before the end of the week the driving test had been passed.

On my return to the hospital, I found I was to work in the Outpatients Department, which included Casualty, and a pleasant surprise came my way when I saw I had been allocated a "superior" room on the fourth floor of Queen Mary's Nurses' Home. It was on the corner of the building and so had two windows and was really quite spacious. There was a worn carpet on the floor (royal blue, of course), a small gas fire, a *wash basin* and the added luxury of an uncomfortable armchair. Buckingham Palace couldn't have been much better, I thought. I was in heaven.

The gas fire proved to be a challenge to light. The gas tap needed to be turned on alongside the fire and time allowed for the gas to come through, after which it had to be lit with a taper or match. If this wasn't done at the crucial moment, it made a frightening "pop" which could singe or burn; and if it wasn't lit at all, you risked poisoning yourself. A bowl of water was already in place which I was told was to humidify the room, but it was not deemed necessary to provide a fire extinguisher.

I unpacked and made my way to the Outpatients. It was a Sunday and I had assumed it would be quiet, but the department looked more like a police station than a hospital. Two large friendly bobbies had removed their helmets and informed me they were guarding a burglar – an old lag already known to the police – who had blown open a safe in a local bank with dynamite. Too late the police had got wind of the planned crime, and the thief's accomplice had managed to scarper. Not so "our" thief. He had been chased on foot until his only route of escape was the canal into which he jumped. He had never learnt to swim; and to add to his woes, he hurt his back badly as he hit the water. He was floundering in the murk when the emergency services arrived and came to his rescue, and he was delivered with efficiency and speed to our hospital for treatment.

Between his moans he confided, 'My missus is in the middle of having a basin of gravy.'

'A basin of *gravy*?' I queried.

'My fifth and her first. I need to have a butcher's hook at the babe. They are at the Wigmore Clinic. I've done them proud. It's costing me forty-seven guineas a week.'

I wasn't surprised he needed to rob a bank.

*

The next day I was assigned to work on the Skin Department which, I was reliably informed, was run by a Sister and her female registrar, one of the very few lady doctors at the hospital. It was rumoured that the couple were in a "relationship". I was taken aside by one more knowledgeable and was told in hushed tones that they were probably lesbians. Still none the wiser, I had to consult a dictionary for clarification.

The bossy and well-endowed Sister was in her fifties, whereas the doctor, who was of a similar age, was a quiet, attractive-looking woman whose neatly plaited hair encircled her head. I never did find out whether the tittle-tattle was true or otherwise, but, whatever the relationship between the two, I felt that *anything* would be an improvement on Sandhurst. And so it proved to be; the two women were delightful, and the atmosphere on the Skin Department was relaxed and informal compared with the required etiquette on the wards.

The senior consultant, the ever-friendly Dr Borrie,

Sister Outpatients and her staff greeting and reassuring the waiting patients.

always thanked me for taking his clinic; Trevor Robinson, his junior registrar, enjoyed a morning cup of tea and a chat when he arrived early to study and was always up for a joke as he removed hundreds of warts; and Dr Green, the elderly part-time dermatologist from Harley Street, turned out to be a potential benefactor.

One of Dr Green's patients was a film star; well, to be honest, nearly a film star. In everyday life, Paul was an aspiring young lawyer, but he also had an ambition to become an actor, and somehow he had managed to land quite a large part in the film *A Taste of Honey.* I tended the dark-haired, handsome young man in the skin clinic along with Dr Green over a period of several weeks. After Paul's discharge from our care, the generous physician said he would like to treat me and a friend to see the film and, as an extra treat, to go out to supper afterwards. It was a throwaway remark and I thought nothing more of it.

*

During the evenings, I worked in the Casualty Department where we had to deal with a variety of cases, some of them truly heartbreaking. On one occasion, I heard the oncoming ringing of the ambulance bell and expected, as was usual, to receive a patient. The doors of the customary white ambulance were opened and a stretchered body completely covered by a sheet was admitted. The BID (Brought in Dead) was a sixty-five-year-old gentleman who was accompanied by an inconsolable middle-aged woman. He was a widower who had been engaged to his forty-year-old fiancée for the past three years, and they were shortly to be wed. The couple had been unable to marry before as, being a dutiful daughter and sister, she had nursed her mother and blind brother, both of whom had since died. This had been the chance for the pair to look to the future, and they had been in a carefree mood as they packed up to go on holiday when he had collapsed and died instantly as he lifted his fiancée's suitcase onto the roof rack of the car.

I stayed with the woman for an hour and a half until her sister arrived to take her home. I held her hand and offered her numerous cups of tea, but I felt totally inadequate. There was nothing I could say or do that could be of any real help; she was beside herself with grief and felt that her life, which early that day had been so full of optimism for the future, had fallen apart forever. She spoke of her fiancé in the present tense as if she couldn't bear his departure. I was just out of my teens and had had no experience of dealing with situations such as this. I found myself on the verge of tears, but it had been drilled into us to never show our emotion and to always remain calm and in control so that we could provide the best possible care to those who needed it. It was, however, often easier said than done.

Tragedy, of course, is an integral component of the day-to-day experiences of working in Casualty; and on another day, very early in the morning, we had a desperate case when a pale young woman of twenty-five, called Sarah, arrived bleeding profusely from her wrists. She was accompanied by a composed-looking man.

I greeted her with, 'Good morning, Sarah. How can we help?'

She was unable to answer and I turned to her companion who, it transpired, was a volunteer from the new organisation called the Samaritans.

'Will you tell the Nurse?' Sarah said in a whisper to him.

He began: 'Sarah's husband attacked her last night, both physically and mentally, and then gave her £2 and told her to get out and find herself somewhere to live. Unfortunately, this resulted in Sarah cutting both her arms with a razor blade.'

Sarah broke in, sobbing, 'I no longer wanted to live, that's why I did it, even though I knew it was against the law to kill myself. I've nothing to live for anymore.'

Once she started talking, she couldn't stop: 'My mum died when I was a baby, and I was put in an orphanage; but Dad took me out when he got married again. But he threw me out of the house a year ago and I had nowhere to go. But last May I met Leon, and we've only been married a few weeks, and now I've been thrown out again.'

In desperation, the exhausted young woman had the foresight to telephone an organisation called the Samaritans in the middle of the night on MAN 9000 for help; one of their volunteers had provided listening support and another accompanied her to hospital.

The bandages round her wrists were sodden with blood, and whilst Sarah's cuts were being sutured in the treatment room, I asked the man about the recently formed charitable organisation which I knew was based nearby. I gathered that the founder of the Samaritans was a vicar called Chad Varah, who had had what he referred to as his "light bulb moment" when he buried a youngster of fourteen who had killed herself because she thought she had a sexually transmitted disease when in fact she had just started her periods.

Varah was aware that in Greater London there were about three suicides a day; and he wondered what and where those in distress were able to go, or to do, if they didn't want to see a doctor or social worker. He felt the answer was an emergency number for people contemplating suicide, but there was no number other than 999.

He was unexpectedly invited to apply for the living of St Stephen Walbrook in the heart of the City of London, and during his interview he told the panel of his "crazy" emergency number telephone scheme; he must have been able to "sell" them the idea as, to give them credit, they thought it was worth a try and he was accepted for the living.

The telephone number of the church turned out, uncannily, to be MAN 9000 which was the one for which Varah had planned to ask. Evidently, publicity for the service was all that was required, and this didn't create a problem for the social vicar – he stood drinks all round for his journalist friends in Fleet Street; and in no time, the calls started pouring in. It didn't take long before it became apparent that Varah couldn't cope with the sheer volume of enquiries on his own; and although he continued to see individuals who needed more than befriending, he selected volunteers who became the listening life-savers. Today, after over sixty years, the organisation is still flourishing and has centres throughout the United Kingdom.

Sarah's volunteer invited me to visit the Crypt at St Stephen, and later I spent some time there. I was full of admiration for the volunteers who provided a twenty-four-hour telephone listening service for those in distress and was grateful that because of them the life of the young, vulnerable wife who had been thrown out of her home had been saved in time.

I attended a couple of training sessions in the Crypt and was very impressed by the dedication of the volunteers, many of whom worked in the city and often covered the night shift after a day's work. Unfortunately, though, it was not possible for me to become a regular volunteer due to my irregular work schedule.

*

On a lighter note, an old woman called Bridie turned up one evening and was evidently a Barts "regular". There were smiles all round as she was cheerily acknowledged, and I was told she just loved coming to the hospital. She always arrived complaining of various symptoms in fairly random areas of her body. Sometimes it was her legs, sometimes her back and sometimes her head. This time, though, it was different.

'It's my tum, nurse,' she said.

'Well, let's get you undressed, shall we, and then the doctor can examine you,' I responded.

Removing her grimy clothes was easier said than done. She had a myriad of overclothes, and when I finally got past these layers, I found several grubby vests under her highly patterned, floral overall. Considering it was her abdomen which was causing her a problem, I decided not to attempt to remove her stockings which were sweaty and smelly and were held up by rubber bands. I was given no choice as to whether or not to remove her knickers as she was knickerless. Although she was filthy, she insisted on inspecting the examination couch and dusted it down with her mauve cardigan before she would deign to lie down. Eventually, she was covered with a hospital blanket and was ready to see the doctor. I folded the covers back, and the doctor rubbed his hands together to warm them, and then he began to palpate Bridie's abdomen.

'Does this hurt, Bridie?' he asked.

'No.'

'And this?'

'No,' she replied.

'Well, what do you think the problem is this time?' he enquired.

'It's my tum, Doctor. I've already told the nurse.'

'Yes, but where is the pain in your tummy?'

She sat up and in her broad Irish accent said, 'It's not *in* my tum; it's my tum,' and she held up an arthritic first digit and gave the thumbs up sign, clearly thinking we were both stupid. She was a lovable rogue, and after finding nothing wrong with her "tum", we fed her and then sent her on her way.

Another recipient of the hospital's hospitality was a dear old man of eighty-six who just turned up one evening. He was seen by the duty doctor, and although he was painfully thin, he was pronounced well enough to go home. But he had no home. He had been sleeping rough under bridges and on the streets and alleyways because he was unhappy in his hostel and was hungry and lonely. We made him scrambled eggs on toast, gave him jelly and ice cream and five shillings, and he was taken back to his hostel by ambulance with a copy of a letter saying someone from the London County Council would call the next day to see about changing his abode.

My time on Outpatients gave me the chance to put one area of my training to the test as I came face-to-face with my first lice infestation. We had learnt during our time at PTS how to catch and treat head lice, nits and pubic lice known as crabs; but in the 1960s, infestations that warranted hospital treatment were surprisingly uncommon. I gowned up and went on a nit hunt with a fine comb and was delighted when I caught my first live louse. Whilst I sympathised with the German girl whose scalp I was waging war with, as she itched and scratched in desperation and rage, I certainly gained a great sense of satisfaction with the mission. A job well done, I decided, as I finished off the task by treating any remaining offending culprits with DDT. By the time I had finished, *my* head itched and *I* scratched continuously over the next few hours. Served me right.

*

My memories of working on Outpatients are ones chiefly of pleasure, apart from the evening when I was the nurse in charge on the Blood Donor Unit. What a night. Everything was going so well, too; blood had been collected efficiently from a multitude of people, and the full bottles had been labelled to perfection.

The last patient of the session, who was a charming woman, was lying back relaxed and happy as she gave her "gift of life".

Strictly speaking, the doctor, Mark Patterson, was not meant to leave the unit until the final procedure had been completed. However, this evening he was keen to get going.

'I'm off,' he said to me. 'Are you all right, Nurse Tisdale?'

'Of course,' I replied with a degree of pride. 'All I have to do is to remove the needle, apply a dressing, give the donor a cup of tea and thank her for coming.' I was glad to be left with this modicum of responsibility.

I removed the needle carefully, applied the dressing and asked the woman to press on it firmly.

'Do you take sugar?' I asked as I turned away to pour out her tea.

'Nurse, it's leaking a bit.'

I glanced over my shoulder and saw blood appearing through the dressing, and then it spurted everywhere – not just a little bit but a lot. My heart started racing, but remembering my First Aid, I didn't panic (much) and I applied firm pressure over the offending bleeding point. *To no effect.* I was faced with a difficult decision. Should I stay with the "patient" to provide reassurance, or should I search for the doctor and leave her on her own to "bleed to death"? I opted to search. Trying to look nonchalant and professional, I walked calmly out of the room and then *ran* for dear life (according to the rules, this was allowed in cases of haemorrhage) in search of the doctor. I found him. What a relief. He was totally unfazed, and all he seemed bothered about was whether I had got a full bottle of blood. He accompanied me back to the "bloody" scene for us to find the "haemorrhage" had ceased and the woman was calmly drinking her cup of tea. How humiliating.

At the end of my time on Outpatients, our set again spent a month in Study Block. This was our last period of study before our dreaded final exams.

As part of the curriculum, I spent a short time attached to a District Nurse and trod the streets of the East End of London. What a worker and what a walker. I felt like a proper District Nurse, in my borrowed gabardine navy mackintosh, as we walked miles from one tenement building to another. I shivered as I spied a rat scrounging around some garbage alongside the mice which were playing unconcernedly in the gutters. There was damp, dingy washing hanging over the shared balconies or draped wherever there was space; there were sniffling babies and children with runny noses; and there were lonely, smelly old people sitting quietly in the walkways as they smoked their Woodbines.

The arrival of the District Nurse was obviously the event of the day. She was a regular visitor, and we were greeted with real pleasure wherever we went. I noticed that in each dwelling the kettle was on the boil. It was so different from working in a hospital where clean bed linen and nightwear were plentiful, all neatly folded and stored in the linen room, always ready for use. On the district we had to bed bath the sick patients and then put the individuals back to bed in their soiled sheets and blankets and often in their damp nightwear as in most cases there was no alternative. We did dressings and injections which were gratefully received, and we were, without exception, offered a cup of tea everywhere we went. The District Nurse advised me to decline as she said when nature called I wouldn't find the toilet facilities very desirable. Good advice. I finished my two days on the district footworn and with blisters but converted to becoming a District Nurse in the future.

As well as lectures and tests during our time in Block, our tutors regaled us with their own experiences. Miss Bailey recounted the time when she was a midwife and dealing with the urine tests of a woman who arrived at the clinic with her bottle of urine. 'Here you are, Nurse, a nice specimen for you,' the woman had proudly announced.

Miss Bailey checked the specimen which was normal apart from one important result. 'You have a lot of sugar in your urine which is somewhat worrying, so I would like you to provide another sample whilst you're here, and we'll also check the sugar content in your blood.'

The tests carried out at the hospital were all normal.

A week later, the patient arrived for another clinic appointment. 'Here you are, Nurse, a nice urine specimen for you.'

Once again, the specimen was loaded with sugar.

Miss Bailey said, 'This is very strange. All your specimens taken at the hospital have been negative. I suppose this specimen *is* yours, isn't it?'

'Oh no,' she replied. 'It's me husband's. Same thing, I thought, as it's his baby as well as mine, and anyway, it was easier for him to pee in the jar.'

*

I was summoned for my "regular" weigh-in whilst we were in Block. Once again I had lost weight, as much as five and a half pounds. I decided that if Ormi asked me if I knew why I had lost weight, I was going to please her by going all starry eyed and revealing that I was "in love". However, she didn't ask me, and I was declared fit; but I was given Cadbury's chocolate powder and she told me to be a good girl and to make myself milky drinks.

We needed the understanding of the Miss Ormistons of this world. Even at the age of twenty, there were times when we yearned to be back in our teens. There were major world events in 1961 which, of course, were worrying, including the Cuban Crisis and the Vietnam War and the commencement of the construction of the Berlin Wall, but selfishly our worries were of a much more personal nature, and current affairs were only gleaned from catching glimpses of the patients' newspapers. I was aware that Russia had sent their first man into space, that the contraceptive pill had been introduced (but only for married women), but regrettably, of most interest to me, was that the Beatles made their first appearance at the Cavern Club in Liverpool and the "*Twist*" started a new craze.

On occasion, several of us would shed our professional image and let off steam by going out dressed as beatniks, wearing black turtleneck sweaters, berets and dark glasses. None of us knew exactly what a beatnik was and what it stood for, and, as far as I can remember, our contribution to the cause was non-existent, but we did our best by climbing on walls, still in disrepair from the war, and trespassing on the decks of deserted barges. Every time we reached a hording, of which there were very many, promoting new constructions by *Trollope and Colls* and *Wimpey*, we would jump in the air, chant the three names and then collapse with laughter. How ridiculous, but somehow it gave us permission to be happy and carefree.

As always, after a month of Block, I was ready to return to proper nursing, and I was looking forward not only to the cheekiness of the "motorbike boys" on the Orthopaedic Ward but also to stepping into "serious" adulthood, as I approached my twenty-first birthday.

Chapter Sixteen

Matilda's Treat

For reasons which I never established, the Orthopaedic Ward was called Henry. Perhaps it was named after the hospital's original benefactor Henry VIII. It was a mixed ward, which in the 1960s was almost unique. However, this wasn't a true mix – it was one ward segregated into a male and a female side; and although the two sexes never met, we had the pleasure of nursing both men and women. The difference in the atmosphere between Henry and Sandhurst had to be experienced to be believed. Before I arrived on the ward, I had already heard stories about the hairy-chested Motorbike Boys from others.

'They're mad caps,' I was told by the blue belt on Henry. 'They are young and fit, but end up in hospital for ages, bedbound due to their multiple fractures. Beware – they are frustrated and flirtatious.'

All this was true; but fortunately, as most of the young men were strung up in various splints and undergoing skeletal traction, we were safe. The work was heavy rather than hard, and there were new methods and procedures to learn:

immobilisation, traction, plaster of Paris, internal methods of fixation and manipulation. There were *Thomas* splints, *Braun's* splints, *gallows* splints and *cock-up* splints, to mention just a few. The wooden splints such as the straight and back splints needed to be padded before use, which involved more sewing. Of course, this landed me in hot water as the ends of the pads had to be *herringbone* stitched; and my sewing, as usual, wasn't up to it. Then there was traction which meant "pulling" and was a process to keep inflamed joint surfaces apart. We were told how the pull was made and maintained. This required an understanding of the mechanical principles involved, chiefly because the weights and pins and pulleys looked (and were) confusing. Apparently, we were told by Miss Hector, females (meaning us student nurses) found the principles difficult to understand, but, she informed us, men (the medical students) had no problem at all. One thing was for certain, with all the splints and pulleys, the ward was always rather untidy.

In addition to all the chaos, there were major bowel difficulties on Henry Ward; this wasn't surprising as most of the patients were long-term and often in bed for months. It became a never-ending topic of conversation, particularly among the men. Young Mike the biker, who never missed a chance to clutch at a nurse with his hairy, muscular arms, hadn't "gone" for several days and was very uptight.

'You've got to give me something. I can't bear it much longer,' he pleaded.

'We could give you a laxative or a suppository or even an enema,' I replied sympathetically but with just a suspicion of a smile. 'Which would you prefer?'

'I don't fancy the suppository and certainly not the enema. How long does the laxative take to work?'

'Five minutes,' I teased. 'Seriously; it will be tomorrow morning.'

I gave him two tablespoons of the thick white Milpar mixed with half a glass of milk. About five minutes later there was a call from Mike's bed. 'Nurse, quick; I need a bedpan.' I marvelled at the value of autosuggestion.

Understandably, the young men had times when they felt depressed and were difficult to manage during their lengthy stay with us. However, hair-washing sessions boosted their morale and were the source of much hilarity. Imagine trying to negotiate all the paraphernalia of the orthopaedic equipment, as well as lifting the mattress two feet over the end of the bed and the placing of a bowl of hot water on a Macintosh on the space made on the metal bedstead; all the while, the six-foot strong men lay back basking. The most important item to make this performance possible was the orange, thick and non-malleable Macintosh, which had to be positioned in a sort of triangular shape to prevent an overflow of water. This delicate placement was the key to success, or otherwise. I cannot recall a time during my hair-washing activities when there was not an immediate flash flood.

The orthopaedic problems of the women patients on Henry Ward couldn't have been more different from those of the men. Broken limbs from motorbike accidents in the women were almost unheard of, but bunion operations were numerous. Mrs Peaker was a delightful "bunion" patient, and she had the added interest of being the aunt of the Attenborough brothers, Richard and David. Even all those years ago, they, along with Richard Attenborough's actress wife Sheila Sim, were famous. I was excited to be introduced to Richard and Sheila, who was looking very glamorous in a fashionable fur stole, and on another occasion, I met David; and when I left his aunt's bedside I heard her say, 'Just look at that 22 inch waist!' I noted he had a very recognisable voice and was charming, but his hair was too long.

As on all the wards, there was a fair amount of coming and going by the consultants, who came to offer their opinions according to their own area of speciality. I had always felt invisible when these great men visited the ward, but shortly after I started on Henry, Dr Borrie was summoned to give advice on one of our patients with a skin complaint. We had been told always to address the consultants as "Sir", and to be respectful, and it was easy to forget that some of the men may actually have seen us as a person beyond the uniform. He recognised me immediately.

'Hello, Nurse, what are you doing here? You should be in my department. Changed from "Outs" to "Ins", have you?' This eminent man had acknowledged me, a mere *student* nurse, making me feel valued and my onlookers envious.

That same day, as I was on my way to lunch, an enormous red Bentley drove into the Square with the semi-retired dermatologist Dr Green behind the wheel. He stopped the car and came over and insisted on giving me the promised £1 to go with a friend to see *A Taste of Honey.* My benefactor had remembered! I recall feeling embarrassed and didn't really like accepting the money, but I didn't wish to offend either. On balance, I decided if he could afford to drive a Bentley then it was likely he could afford to treat a couple of student nurses, and I thanked him gratefully.

As well as the £1 there were other unsolicited gifts that came my way. Three large blocks of Cadbury's milk chocolate arrived from David to fatten me up, and Priscilla had put a parcel, wrapped beautifully in silver paper, on my bed. There was a long-stemmed rose lying on the top of the package under which was a written message – *I used to wear this when I went out with Michael, and now I'm not, I no longer want to wear it. I would like to give it to you as I think your love is genuine.* Inside the parcel was some half-used "In Love" soap, the remains of some perfume and an almost full pink, heart-shaped container of hand lotion – all under the name of Norman Hartnell the Queen's dressmaker. I was really touched.

Priscilla, Anna, Meg, Mary and Anne were now with me in another Nurses' Home which was in Charterhouse Square. We had all moved several months earlier before we started Block, into the rather grand but dilapidated building which was situated near Smithfield Meat Market and was only a few minutes' walk from the hospital. No longer did I have my rather grand bedroom in Queen Mary's Nurses' Home, but on the plus side, Meg and I had adjoining rooms which made for a different kind of comfort. Beth, now three sets behind us due to her tuberculosis and more recent appendectomy, wasn't, unfortunately, with us. Meg and I had a glimmer of how the other half, or rather one percent, lived, when we were passing Matron's flat one evening. We found the good woman stranded at her open door dressed in a dusty pink, quilted dressing gown with curlers in her hair. No longer did she look important, but she had the appearance of an ordinary woman. She had mislaid her keys earlier which she had now fortuitously found. The "thief", she told us, was none other than her black poodle who had carried the self-same keys onto his lavatory (a pile of newspaper). Usually, this would have been the end of the story, but apparently Matron had sent Miss Ormiston off on a fruitless search to her office to look for them. Now she was in a quandary as she couldn't go and look for Ormi due to her state of undress. We, naturally, volunteered to deliver the good news. So grateful was Matron that we were invited into her inner sanctum to view the exact situation of the missing keys. We had a good look at her flat whilst we were about it and decided it was without style and rather boring.

For the first time since PTS we all enjoyed being in the same sleeping quarters together and met up in one or other of our bedrooms for a nightcap. Whenever possible, Beth joined us to enjoy a cup of coffee whilst we chatted incessantly about our various patients. One evening, Mary came off her ward having been charmingly entertained by a story she had overheard about a little boy who was writing about the "facts of life", which she couldn't resist repeating.

'Mummy, where did Granny come from?'

'Oh, a stork brought her,' replied his mother.

'So where did *you* come from?' he persisted.

'Another stork brought me.'

Finally, he asked, 'Where did *I* come from?'

'Oh, a little stork brought you,' she said proudly.

The little boy said nothing, but wrote in his essay that there had been no natural births in his family for three generations.

Beth was also a good storyteller and regaled us with many tales. One of these related to a little Welsh lady of seventy-eight who was of "good breeding" but had an aversion to drinking. This did not mean she was an avowed teetotaler but rather that she refused to drink the required amount of fluid per day which was considered particularly important due to the nature of her complaint. Everything was tried to tempt her to drink – tea, coffee, milk, water, soup, fruit juices and every other existing liquid, but she staunchly refused to drink more than two cupfuls a day. Battle commenced, and the nurses had to practically force a glassful of liquid down the patient's protesting throat. The next morning, there was a neatly written notice on her bedside locker:

I beg the nurses' pardon for being so troublesome, but I find it impossible to drink. You may regard this in the nature of an uncooperative strike. I am sorry.

Signed Iris Jones

Needless to say, Miss Jones was no longer asked to drink, and she made an excellent recovery without the extra fluids.

*

Life certainly wasn't all about work on the wards, and I had a big decision to make. Should I, or should I not, attempt to knit a jumper for David for Christmas? This was tricky because I lacked, as you may have now realised, the necessary expertise, and I was also short of time as it was already the 7th October. Nevertheless, I bought a knitting pattern and "mountains" of Moss Green wool and a pair, as far as I can remember, of Number 11 knitting needles. So far so good.

The pattern seemed simple enough: Purl 2, Knit 2, Purl back; Purl 2, Knit 2, Purl back; etc, etc. Even *I* could manage this, surely? There was a problem, however. I couldn't remember how to cast the stitches on. Head Girl Jane came to the rescue and promised to "do" the neck when the time came and also to attach the sleeves to the body of the potential garment. With much unpicking and redoing, the attractive pattern slowly emerged, and the growing pieces rested happily between rows in my basket over the next few months. But the question remained – would I ever get the wretched jumper finished for Christmas?

During our off duty, we enjoyed various activities, particularly at the new Gloucester House swimming pool. Swimming galas proved the perfect spectator sport. The wearing of swimming costumes had a wonderful way of appearing to minimise seniority among the nursing staff. On one occasion, Prilli, the slender beauty, was up against the fulsome Sister Lawrence. Not to be outdone, Prilli stuffed a scarf into the top of her bathing costume to give her the appearance of strength and endowment. As was usual with Prilli's exploits, this was not an unmitigated success as the scarf came adrift, shot across the pool and became lodged in the outlet pipe. She managed (again, as usual) to get away with it as no one put two and two together.

Beth and I enjoyed supper at John O's flat. John O was a close friend of mine from home and had been one of our hosts when Beth and I had gone to Cambridge. He was a medical student and was now doing his clinical training at St Thomas's. But it was his flatmate, a Chinese student, who impressed us – not only had he bought the food for our supper, but he had purchased both meat and fish because, he said, he didn't know our religious beliefs.

John's cousin Bill was also very thoughtful and generous when one day he spotted me as I was buying a ticket at the railway station in Leamington Spa for Paddington. We were both travelling to London from our Warwickshire homes, and he insisted on buying me a First Class ticket. I had never travelled First Class before, and I didn't suppose I was likely to again. It was exceedingly plush; we were treated to a full English breakfast with the attendants managing to serve eggs, bacon, sausage, tomato, mushrooms and black pudding with expertise despite the rocking of the train, and I found the whole experience thoroughly enjoyable. What luxury!

However, I was brought down to earth when Meg, Mary, Beth, Anna and I went to *The Sound of Music,* starring Jean Bayliss, back then a fairly unknown actress. We managed to get cheap tickets at six shillings each, which meant we were seated right at the back and at the side of the auditorium where we couldn't really see, but it was still worth it.

The entertainment sometimes found its way into our on-duty lives, too, and there was great excitement when the hospital was contacted by the Temperance Seven who offered to give a free performance to the patients and to the medical and nursing staff. We couldn't believe it, *The Temperance Seven*? They were *famous*. The group, who were founded in 1955 by students at the Chelsea School of Art and specialised in 1920s style jazz music, were all the rage in 1961 and had recently appeared at the London Palladium and had taken part in the Royal Variety performance. The concert, which was held on Tuesday 19th December in Gloucester House Hall, was a resounding success; and they played their Number 1 hit *You're Driving Me Crazy* and *Pasadena*, which went on to be Number 4 in the UK Singles Chart.

It was around this time that I first met Matilda. She had been transferred from the Royal Marsden Hospital and it was she, perhaps more than any other patient during my training, who had such a profound and lasting effect on me.

Matilda arrived on Henry Ward on the afternoon of Saturday, 2nd December, 1961. She was a fifteen-year-old black girl with eyes like saucers, a toothy grin and a mop of fuzzy hair tamed into miniature braids, held in place by a multitude of scarlet ribbons. She acknowledged me with a cheerful smile that vanished momentarily as she explained that her father, who was a widower, had had to return to Ghana temporarily to look after the rest of his large motherless family. Matilda was therefore on her own in a strange country.

The obviously bright and well-educated youngster had a sarcoma (bone cancer) and had been admitted to Barts to have her right leg and hind quarter amputated. She was noticeably in continuous pain, but she never grumbled; and in the lead-up to her operation we spent much time together and became the greatest of friends.

Her pain was worse when she was moved, and she always wanted to talk to us as we gave her a bed bath to try and take her mind off her agony. She was particularly keen to chat about Christmas.

'What do your family do on Christmas Day?' I asked.

'We eat Big Chicken Soup with soda-pop drinks. It's always chicken at Christmas, and we always have fufu.' Her eyes lit up as she spoke.

'What's fufu?' I enquired.

'We make fufu by pounding the cassava plant and unripe plantain together with a little water for a long time until it is a smooth paste, then we put it in a big bowl and make little balls of the mixture with our fingers before we dip them in the soup. It's delicious.'

I felt I should change the topic of conversation as I could see I had inadvertently made Matilda homesick, but she smiled and said it made her happy talking about home as she continued.

'"Afenshia paaooh" is the greeting we use at Christmas, and you would reply "Afe nko eme to yen bio", which means "Hope to see you next year".'

I did my best, without success, to repeat the words after Matilda, and at least we had distracted her sufficiently to give her a bed bath without her suffering too much discomfort. She looked so little and vulnerable as we replaced the cradle on the bed to keep the bedclothes off her legs.

On the day of her operation, I helped Matilda into her white gown and replaced her bed clothing with two red theatre blankets. She was brave; but as she looked at me, the smile that was usually on her lips faltered. Then the pre-operative injection thankfully made her drowsy. I was relieved when the operating theatre orderlies arrived and lifted Matilda carefully on the canvas stretcher and onto the trolley. She had asked if I could accompany her to the anaesthetic room, a request to which Sister agreed. This was a privilege and the least I could do, but it was almost too painful to bear. I held her hand as the very kindly anaesthetist inserted the needle gently into her vein and she drifted off to sleep.

The operation went as well as could be expected and Matilda progressed well post-operatively, although she was still in a lot of discomfort.

'I'm really lucky, you know,' she said when the pain had diminished a little.

'Why's that?' I enquired, as I was doing my best to brush the tangles out of her now un-braided hair.

'Well, I've still got one leg. Some people have lost both of theirs.'

I couldn't reply for fear of my voice faltering.

Finally, 20th December arrived. Christmas was on the horizon, and it was time for Matilda to return to the Royal Marsden, and I was to escort her on her journey. It was about 5pm when the ambulance arrived, so it was already dark when we left. We went via Holborn, past Gamages and headed off towards the West End when much to Matilda's and my surprise, the ambulance suddenly came to a halt. We looked at each other. What was going on? Had there been an accident? We were both puzzled. The two back doors suddenly swung open and simultaneously the two middle-aged ambulancemen stood to attention and with big smiles on their faces saluted Matilda. We were in Regent Street, in the middle of the road, holding up all the traffic. Without a word, the men covered Matilda with an extra blanket and then lifted her on her stretcher, out of the ambulance and way above, so she could see the magnificent Christmas lights lighting up one of the most well-known streets of the world.

'LOOK!' she cried. 'LOOK! There are huge illuminated crowns! There are lighted lanterns! There are twinkling stars.' She could hardly contain herself and

Christmas lights in Regent Street 1961. (Reproduced by kind permission of Getty Images.)

kept saying, 'Oh look, Nurse Tizzy, LOOK – it's so beautiful. I've never seen anything like it!'

The motorists and taxi drivers could see what was going on and there were calls of 'Merry Christmas! Merry Christmas!' and not a horn was blown with irritation or impatience.

The kindness of the ambulance drivers was re-enacted in Oxford Street, and again Matilda was joyful. This time, the lights were different, and again the drivers in their static cars waited patiently. I saw London and Londoners in a new light that evening; and I will never, ever forget the look of pleasure on Matilda's face.

When we arrived at the Royal Marsden, she turned to me and said, 'I'm missing my Barts nurses already.'

I didn't stay long. She whispered, 'Afenshia paaooh' and I tried my best to reply 'Afe nko eme to yen bio,' but I was too overcome with emotion, and instead I gave her a big hug and left with tears in my eyes. I never saw her again. In spite of the amputation, the cancer had already spread, and sadly she had less than three months to live, but our trip and her treat had been filled with happiness and joyful memories, all thanks to those thoughtful ambulancemen.

*

In the run-up to Christmas, as a surprise for my parents, I had a black and white photograph taken of me in my uniform, knowing it would give them pleasure to display it proudly on their piano. This time, though, unlike the one taken by the photographer at PTS, I made sure my cap was perched towards the back of my head and my hair was definitely not behind my ears but curled smoothly round my face, "Hollywood" style. I felt the photo needed to attempt to make me look pretty rather than puritanical. At least that was one present sorted, but, in early

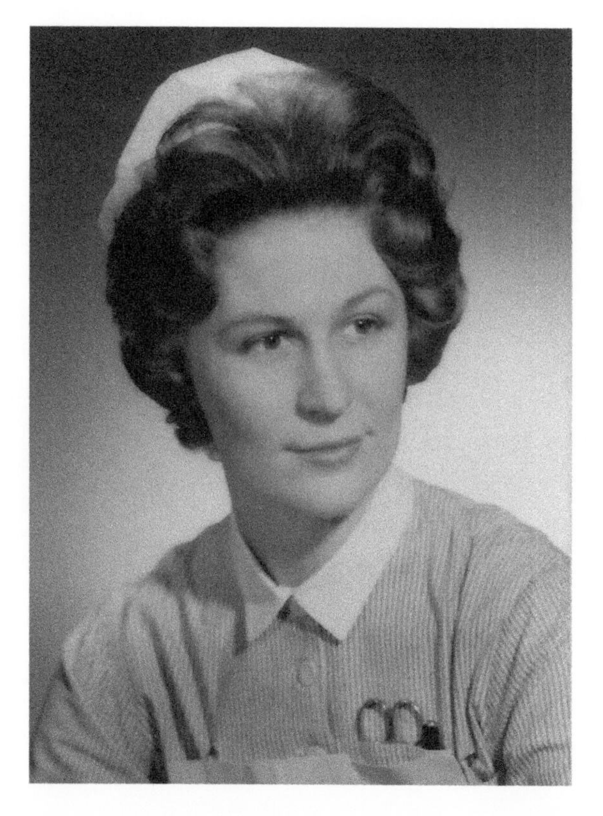

Trying to achieve the film star look.

December, I was still knitting furiously. Only half of the second sleeve to do.

There were many twenty-first birthdays for the girls in our set in 1961, and they were all, one by one, duly celebrated. Then it was my turn, and it was truly memorable. I was "bumped" for the first time in my life, before being greeted by staff and patients on Henry Ward who were singing *Happy Birthday* with gusto. An array of gifts awaited me on the table in the ward kitchen: a tin of Tweed talcum powder, Tweed perfume and (would you believe) *Tweed* bath salts, each with the brand's distinctive and unforgettable sickly scent, as well as a plant and a dog made out of marzipan. What more could I have wanted?

John O drove me home in a dense fog and gave me a beautifully wrapped bracelet. When I eventually arrived home, there were more presents, including a gold bracelet from David – unwrapped.

*

The knitting marathon was nearly over, and at last I handed the front, back and sleeves to Jane so she could complete the *amazing* garment, which I may add was in service for nigh on twenty years. As I admired it, I began to look forward to 1962 and what it might bring.

Chapter Seventeen

Hauled Over the Coals

On Sunday, 21st January, 1962, after a few false starts, David located my father in the attic of our house, who was immersed in putting the finishing touches to one of his oil paintings.

'Could I have a word with you, Mr Tisdale?' he called from below.

'Come on up, David; but be careful, the ladder's quite tricky.'

David wasn't one for heights. However, love won through, and he managed the marathon climb before negotiating the top step of the folding ladder and falling at my father's feet.

I, of course, wasn't party to the conversation that ensued, but of course, I had an inkling as to its subject matter. Meanwhile, my mother was becoming suspicious of the shenanigans above and arrived at the bottom of the ladder to find my father discreetly but energetically pointing at the fourth finger of his left hand.

'What on earth does that mean, George?'

Then suddenly she realised the significance of his mime. For some reason, known only to herself, all she could think of

My parents were delighted to agree to my engagement.

saying was, 'I'll have to get my hair done,' although quite what that had to do with my engagement we never did find out.

Congratulations all round and I was now formally engaged; but a day later, reality hit when I had to catch the train back to London to start my next period of night duty about which, for good reason, I was exceedingly apprehensive.

Naturally, I was thrilled to be engaged, and I was delighted with my traditional, three-diamond ring which fitted snugly on the third finger of my left hand. Going back to the hospital also gave me the opportunity to show off the evidence of my betrothal to anyone who showed even the slightest bit of interest, but there was still work to be done.

The men's medical ward called Smithfield was my next placement. The names Smithfield and Barts had been intertwined since time immemorial, when legend had it that St Bartholomew had commanded the monk Rahere to build a hospital and church at Smithfield in 1123. Rahere was a bright and persuasive individual and having been a former court entertainer, was able to gain permission from King Henry I to build on the land. Not only this, he also managed to obtain a charter to hold an annual fair on Saint Bartholomew's Feast Day on 24th August every year to raise money for the running of the hospital.

The fair was originally held in the precincts of the priory where Rahere enjoyed showing off his juggling skills, and later, as it expanded, it moved into the open space of Smithfield and became the country's largest cloth fair and London's biggest annual celebration. Smithfield over the centuries became synonymous with revelry, debauchery, violence and, of course, meat.

Smithfield "the ward", however, was not a place of revelry – it was for the care and nurture of sick men with a variety of medical conditions. This time, my three months of night duty was to be spent as the Night Staff and so I would be in charge of twenty-six patients once the Twilight Nurse left at midnight.

I enjoyed the process of "doing the round" each evening and speaking to every patient individually and enquiring how they were feeling. Eerily, an unforeseen event took place a few days after I had started on the ward. As usual, I greeted all the patients, including Mr Ernest Stubbington, a seventy-eight-year-old widower who had terminal cancer. I noticed his "sun spotted" hands which were resting peacefully on the counterpane, and as I arrived at his bed, he lifted a trembling hand slowly in recognition and gave me a bright smile.

'Good evening, Mr Stubbington. How have you been today?'

'Not bad, Nurse. Not bad. Thank you, Nurse,' he replied.

After our pleasantries, I asked him if he would like his usual tot of brandy as a nightcap. He lifted the same frail arm and whispered, 'I have to tell you something, Nurse. Although I haven't felt any worse today than I have before, I have a hunch that I will die tonight.'

Naturally, I felt very uneasy, and, after saying a few reassuring words to him, I reported his worrying premonition to the Twilight Nurse. Mr Stubbington was a sick man, of that there was no doubt, but it was not felt he was at risk of an imminent death. We both did our best to reassure him, but he seemed resigned and content to face what he thought was going to be his probable fate. We kept very regular checks on him, and it was noticeable that his temperature was below normal and his hands and feet felt cold, but otherwise he was sleeping peacefully. At 1.35am, his pulse could no longer be felt and his breathing had ceased. His hunch was uncanny. It was hard to know what to make of it. The important lesson I took from the sad event was always to take a patient's premonitions seriously as there were some things that seemed to be beyond medical science or understanding.

Mr Stubbington's death was the first for which I had to assume total responsibility during my spell on Smithfield Ward, and I was grateful to have an excellent junior working with me as we performed the last offices. I always felt it was a debatable privilege to carry out this final duty for a patient. Mr Stubbington's body was prepared in readiness to be taken to the mortuary chapel, where his relatives would be visiting the next day; and it was important that their last impression of him should be one of peace and serenity. Although the laying out of the very sick and elderly was a solemn procedure, it was not always, or necessarily, a sad one. Sometimes we would feel grateful that the patient had finally been relieved of their suffering. It was very different when a child or young person died, and my faith was always sorely challenged at their premature deaths. Thankfully, I never had to carry out the last offices for the young without being paired with a senior staff nurse or Sister, and whilst Mr Stubbington's death was sad, he had had a good long life which had drawn to its inevitable conclusion. During these times, I don't remember ever giving my own demise a single thought; it felt too far in the future to be relevant.

After we had laid out Mr Stubbington and the formalities had been completed, his death was reported to the Steward's office by the Night Sister, so the Steward, Mr Antony Brett, could inform the relatives and could assist them with any funeral arrangements to be made. I was in awe of Mr Brett, who had a very senior role at Barts and was responsible for the general management of the hospital, and I knew Mr Stubbington's relations would be regarded by him as his "guests" and he would do all he could to help.

Although there were several Night Sisters, Miss Russell was the Night Superintendent and it was she who was in overall charge of the hospital at night and carried responsibility for all the sick patients. She terrified us. Her tongue was as sharp as a razor; and over the next few months I was to find out whether she really was the tyrant hospital legend had us believe or not.

Miss Russell was always referred to as "Jane", after Jane Russell the sex symbol of the 1940s, but anybody less like the film star would have been hard to find. *Our* "owl-like" Jane was pale, tiny in stature and skeletal. Probably the only resemblance to her namesake was that they were both creatures of the night. *Our* Jane had the eyes of a cat; we were convinced she could see in the dark, and she also had acute hearing. It was reliably reported she could hear a teaspoon drop in a ward when she was two floors above. She shone her torch every night in the ward kitchen to check no houseman had been secreted away; and if she caught us wearing a cardigan to keep warm during the night, we were in for big trouble. *Our* Jane was feared, but, as I was soon to learn, she was also revered.

We met for the first time several days after I had become engaged when she arrived on Smithfield Ward to receive the night report. By this time, the continual putting on and taking off of my engagement ring, so it could be pinned behind the bib of my apron when I was on duty, had left me with a very sore, inflamed finger as the jeweller had made the ring a little too small. So, I had ended up under Miss Ormiston's care, and Miss Russell spied my bandage.

'What's that, Nurse? What have you done to yourself?' she demanded.

'I've just become engaged, Miss Russell, and my ring was too tight.'

'You must be mad. You're going to marry a medical man, I suppose?'

'No, Miss Russell, he is not medical.'

'Well, you must be marrying a man in a million then. You're a sensible child after all.'

I had several nerve-racking experiences with Miss Russell during my time on Smithfield. Prior to her arrival on the ward, to receive the night report, I always worked hard to master and memorise the twenty-six names of all the patients and their various diagnoses and treatments. Miss Russell, fierce and dignified, sat on a chair at Sister's desk, blinking under the light of the anglepoise lamp, and I sat to her left on a stool. One night, everything seemed to be going according to plan and I was able to give fairly comprehensive information about all the patients until I made a big mistake.

'Mr Evans has been no trouble at all,' I reported.

'No trouble?' She was ablaze with fury. 'How *dare* you?'

I looked at her in complete surprise.

She was off and she didn't stop.

Why did I think patients were admitted to hospital? What did I think I was doing if he was "no trouble"? Patients were meant to be a trouble or otherwise they wouldn't be in hospital. Hadn't I learnt anything at all since I had started my training?

I was flabbergasted and somewhat confused as I felt I had been correct in my assumption and he truly had been "no trouble", but that wasn't good enough for Miss Russell.

The next night was no better. I started the report at 1am, and as I delivered details and progress of the patients in the hushed ward of the sleeping men, a sudden rasping sound came from the top left of the ward and then a flash of light.

'That noise, Nurse Tisdale, in case you didn't know, is the sound of a match being lit,' Miss Russell said sharply.

My heart sank. I knew who the culprit was immediately.

'Well, Miss Russell, Mr Hopkin is an alcoholic, and he says the only way he can manage without his alcohol is to smoke,' I said defensively.

She would have none of my excuses, and she spent the next twenty minutes haranguing me for *his* wrongdoing and said that it was the governors who made the rules and not student nurses and she would be reporting me to Matron in the morning.

Meanwhile, the transgressor peacefully finished smoking his cigarette.

Miss Russell arrived on the ward for her second visit at 4.45am. 'Have you licked your wounds?' she asked me.

'Still licking,' I replied, much to her amusement.

On her final visit at 7.20am, she came up to me, looked me up and down and then said, 'Have you been good?'

'I have, Miss Russell.'

I caught a glimmer of a smile before she said, 'You're a good girl really, and I have to scratch at you all sometimes.'

Of course, she never did report me to Matron. I don't think she reported anybody, ever. She had no need; her threat was sufficient.

Miss Russell was sometimes unreasonable and impossible, but in the end, we all worshipped the ground she walked on. She was truly one of the old school, and there is no doubt she *was* a legend; and despite her sharp tongue, she inspired loyalty and was often thoughtful to her nurses.

I will never forget the night we had a very sick young man called Roger on the ward who was dying of kidney disease. He was asking for more morphia to ease his pain, and it was agreed with the doctors that this should be given and that it was likely to be his final injection. Miss Russell took me to one side.

'This painkiller,' she said, 'is likely to be Roger's last.'

She would not allow me to give the injection and instead gave it to him herself. My relief was immense.

Two hours later, the terminally ill young patient slipped peacefully away. Miss Russell had the heart and the courage of a lion – she had both aided and eased Roger's death. I was so grateful to her on two accounts. She had relieved a patient's suffering before it had become impossibly unbearable, and she had understood my anxiety that in giving the injection I would have precipitated his death. She was a true inspiration.

Not so, Sister Smithfield. The next morning, I was in hot water from the moment she arrived at 7.50am, chiefly for not having made up Roger's notes. This felt very unfair as we had a full ward and we *had* managed to make all twenty-six beds before the day staff arrived on duty. I had already been in trouble with her the previous morning relating to Roger's care when, on the houseman's orders, I had given the patient a drug called paraldehyde and she said it was unacceptable and I was only to follow her instructions. There seemed no way to get it right.

*

One of the important traditions at the hospital was the saying of prayers before the patients settled for the night. This was very special for those of us with a strong Christian belief; but even for those without a faith, this universal custom was not only well accepted but welcomed. On some wards, the Sisters took the prayers before going off duty; and on others, the Senior Night Nurse was asked to say them. Although it was allowable to use different prayers, the same one was always included; and although short, it was appropriate and much appreciated by the patients:

Lighten our darkness, we beseech thee, O Lord; and by thy great mercy defend us from all perils and dangers of this night; for the love of thy only Son, our Saviour, Jesus Christ. Amen

There were nearly always a small number of patients on the ward who belonged to different denominations, and quite frequently these were from the Jewish faith. Inevitably, there were times when one of them died, and if the patient was an orthodox Jew we adhered to the strict Jewish observances. If any procedure was necessary, we preserved the dignity and honour of the patient by wearing gloves and by touching the patient as little as possible. We didn't wash the deceased but covered the body and left it untouched so the last offices could be performed by a Jewish undertaker.

*

It was cold sitting at Sister's desk writing the night report.

We had a job keeping warm at night; and even in the bitterly cold weather, the wearing of cardigans on the ward was forbidden. I hated being cold, so once a week there was a treat to behold when the two duty beds on the ward were kept warm with an electric blanket ready to receive emergency patients. Countless times in the middle of the night and wearing only my short-sleeved cotton uniform dress, I went to the beds and put my arms under the warm covers and vowed I would even be prepared to have my little finger chopped off if only I could crawl into the lovely warm nest. Fortunately, by the morning I had warmed up and the vow no longer held. Paula said she prayed Night Sister would take pity on her and would tell her to tuck up in the cosy warmth – a prayer which, however fervently said, was never answered.

Melvyn, on the other hand, was a patient who was never cold at night. He was a young man in his twenties with very severe, widespread psoriasis [a skin condition], and he couldn't sleep because he itched and was so hot that he continually threw off his bedcovers. Throughout the night, Melvyn would repeatedly ask us to make him some sandwiches. This was all well and good, until we realised that every time we delivered his request to the bedside, he had an extremely visible erection which was very embarrassing for us, but he seemed quite happy as he munched away.

Some nights, we were exceedingly busy; and on one night, never to be forgotten, we had to put up extra beds, and we admitted five duty cases of which three of the patients were severely ill. There were only two of us to cope for twelve long hours, with not only the emergencies, but also the routine ward duties as well. One of the patients who arrived in the early hours seemed relatively stable until, without warning, he tried to get out of bed and collapsed to the floor unconscious. This woke several nearby patients who called for urgent help. I was on the other side of the ward dealing with another patient when I heard their cries – an absolute rule throughout the hospital was that the ward should *never* be without one nurse in attendance and I was on the spot without delay. I was sure the patient had had a heart attack, and in the darkness of the sleeping ward, I knelt by his side and started resuscitation as we had been instructed in the classroom. I was certain the man was dying. All of a sudden, the beam from a torch shone on the dramatic scene.

'What's going on here, Nurse Tisdale?' It was the calm voice of Miss Miles, the young Sister who had seen us through PTS.

She took a close look at the patient and felt his pulse. 'I don't think this gentleman requires resuscitation. You can stop now, Nurse.'

She was right. The patient slowly recovered consciousness before vomiting a copious amount of blood *everywhere,* and Miss Miles commented it looked like a scene from the popular soap opera on television called *Emergency Ward 10.*

I was mortified. I had not played *my* part well, but the next day was even more humiliating. I was heralded by the patient's family, who had been notified by the other patients, as the one who had saved their relative's life, and I was presented with a box of chocolates and a pair of black Aristoc stockings. I could only be grateful; but save his life, I did not.

Shortly after the *Emergency Ward 10* debacle, my time on Smithfield came to an end, and during my last report, Sister managed a smile; and a lovely one it was too.

*

Time rushed by, and in early March everyone in our set had to pay their examination fee of four guineas for the state finals. Unfortunately, one member had some shattering news. She had become pregnant and had been ordered to leave immediately. The poor girl was therefore unable to sit both the state and hospital examinations. Pregnancy in a student nurse was a reason for immediate dismissal.

As far as I was concerned, there was no question of becoming pregnant. Unlike the sexually liberated society of today, in the 1960s, virginity was still cherished by many; and for me, sexual intercourse and any resulting pregnancy was going to have to wait until after I was married.

However, I wanted to get married and the sooner the better – I was in love, for goodness' sake, but I was faced with a problem. If I married before *completing* my fourth year at the hospital, I would not receive my coveted Barts badge or be eligible to join the League of Barts Nurses which was founded by Matron Isla Stewart in 1899 and which was renowned for being the first organisation of its kind in the United Kingdom. But could I wait that long to marry? My mind was distracted somewhat when I received a letter from Walter, the schoolmaster, who wrote professing undying love, but he was too late.

Chapter Eighteen

Bitter Sweet

Kenton was also a ward with a reputation, but I decided I could stand anything having been submitted to, and survived, the wrath of both Sister Sandhurst and Sister Smithfield. I was prepared.

Sister Kenton was yet another dedicated spinster who rarely went off duty and was known to be tough and uncompromising. She had little time for nurses who were not good with "her" little patients and said she could spot within minutes a nurse's intrinsic ability to get on with children or not. She was often frantic, very excitable and frequently bad-tempered, but she was a superb nurse. Her knowledge was astounding, and the children under her care were very much her priority in life. She would do anything for her small charges and indeed did – on her retirement, a surviving conjoined twin, a young girl, lived with her for many years. Sister Kenton would never have chosen to be a Matron or to work in administration. In her view she had trained so she could *nurse*; somebody else could be responsible for running the institution. Matron gave her Sisters considerable independence, and Sister Kenton took advantage of this trust and was able to have a free rein and managed Kenton Ward as she pleased.

A new shift system came into operation whilst I was on Kenton. This meant we either started at 7.30am and finished at 3.30pm, or we started at 1pm and finished at 9pm. The Hospital Final Examinations and the State Examinations loomed ever nearer; and unfortunately, like Sandhurst, the children's ward had an internal night duty rota. I was worried the exams and night duty would coincide, but there was little I could do about it.

Working on Kenton was a joy, but to be honest it suited me better when Sister wasn't around. She was a tricky customer and we had our ups and downs as happened one day when she told me off as I had never been told off before.

I was the designated "barrier" nurse for a blind, nine-month-old baby called Simon who had had gastroenteritis. His condition required a special nursing technique called Barrier Nursing which had to be carried out to prevent the spread of infection to others. Sister took me aside.

'Nurse Tisdale, I want to watch you measure Simon's feed. I then want to watch you gown up, go into the baby's cubicle, insert the oesophageal tubing and then feed the baby at *exactly* 2pm this afternoon. Is that understood?'

I spent the morning worrying about the timings for the baby's feed, and when five minutes to two arrived I began to panic. Two o'clock came and Sister was nowhere to be seen. I was the most senior nurse on duty, and I had no one from whom to take advice. So, what should I do? Should I make the baby wait past the allotted time, or should I continue without Sister?

I decided the patient must come first. So, I measured the feed, prepared the tray with its feeding tube, washed my hands and carefully put on the gown and mask. Still no Sister. It was now 2.10pm.

I pulled back the pale blue screen curtains, on which frolicked my favourite Beatrix Potter characters, and decided I must have the courage of my convictions and continue. I passed the oesophageal tube into the baby's stomach, checked it was in the right place, and then attached the glass container to the tube and added the milk. It was quite simple; I completed the task with some satisfaction and much relief.

At 2.25pm, Sister stormed on the ward, incandescent with rage. Her eyes narrowed and her voice went up a decibel. 'I told you I wanted to watch you through the whole process. Get out of my sight!'

I had made the wrong decision. I should have waited.

I wasn't the only one making mistakes on Kenton Ward. Prilli, the blonde, also had a close shave when, one weekend, she boiled the babies' teats dry in Sister's very special small saucepan. Smoke poured out of the window causing passersby to notify the hospital. Apparently, the beleaguered girl redecorated the ward kitchen before Sister came on duty on the Monday morning and managed to get away with it, as only Prilli could.

The responsibility for the little lives rested overall, of course, with Sister. The ward specialised in childhood cancers, and death was never far away. It was incredibly hard to see the very sick children and babies, as well as the anguish on the faces of their parents. For many of these small patients there was little or no hope; and Sister encouraged us to play with the children both on the ward and in the Square, where they enjoyed dipping their hands in the water around the fountain. There was no free visiting for parents unless the circumstances were exceptional, and although there were nearly always tears when parents left after visiting hours, it was astonishing to see how, in a very short time, children could be distracted and peace prevailed. There was much laughter and fun in spite of the sadness.

There were lots of happy faces around the fountain.

The St Bartholomew's Women's Guild ran the Children's Library, and Lady Bodley Scott, the organiser and wife of Sir Ronald Bodley Scott, worked tirelessly and happily to keep the children occupied. Some of the children were too young or too ill to read by themselves, and there was a special little chap called Ginger of whom one could only see a great tuft of carroty hair and blue eyes above the sheet, who fell into this category.

Lady Bodley Scott sat on Ginger's bed reading *Noddy and Big Ears in Toyland* by Enid Blyton.

'Well, that's the end of the chapter, Ginger,' she said. 'Do you want some more?'

He nodded.

Another chapter was read. 'Do you *still* want some more?' He nodded again.

This one-sided conversation went on until Lady Bodley Scott had finished the whole book. In an unguarded moment, she said, 'Well, did you like the story then?'

The little patient enjoying the bike in spite of having radiotherapy.

The answer came in a rich adenoidal cockney: 'It's not the story I loike. I loikes listening to you, lady. You talks so funny.'

The children sometimes became confused as to "who was who" on the ward, and Lady Bodley Scott arrived one morning to be greeted by a cheeky little five-year-old called Peter who rushed up to her and demanded to know, 'Are you a mum, a nurse or *what*?'

Lady Bodley Scott said it was such a pleasure to be greeted by children such as Peter, to receive a gay smile from an old friend or to see the tremulous smile of a very shy child who would be a friend of the future.

The helpers in the Children's Library were constantly asked by the boys for "something funny". Lady Bodley Scott decided that her job was to amuse or to educate, so she did her best to oblige and decided that annuals were her best bet, but she got it wrong – they meant comics. However, she was very heartened when a little girl of eight asked for a book on nursing.

*

On 4th May, we celebrated our third anniversary, and Beth and I agreed that the day would forever be imprinted on our minds whatever we may be doing in the future; and since then on each anniversary we have been in touch with each other, happily reminiscing.

On the anniversary itself, Beth, Meg, Priscilla, Anna, Mary, Anne and I met up for a commemorative "tea" party after we had come off the early duty. This was held in the Nurses' Home at Charterhouse Square, and Anne had commandeered a small table on which she had put a white linen and lace tablecloth as well as china cups, saucers and small plates, all of which had probably belonged to her mother. She served delectable, softly boiled eggs accompanied by delicate, of course, crustless brown bread and butter and had made China tea which was poured from a matching teapot. We felt we had become quite sophisticated in our maturing years – no longer did we toast each other with fizzy lemonade – but we *did* have a little party piece; so, with apologies to Rudyard Kipling:

If you can walk with quiet tread
And not a soul disturb,
If you can take all insults
And still your temper curb,
If you can tidy beds all day
And rub backs till they shine,
If you can empty bedpans
When you're about to dine,
If you can rearrange your cap
With one hand in the sluice,
Or make a man a fruit drink
When there isn't any juice,
If you can look at Matron
Without a baleful glare
When she comes on her daily round
And says 'Nurse, what dreadful hair!'
If you can get your exams first time,
Without the slightest struggle,
Or set up for an I/V drip

And not get in a muddle...
If you can do all these things
And never once feel faint,
You'll never make a nurse, my dear –
You'll be a blinking saint!

And so said all of us.

As I had feared, I was on night duty as the examinations approached, and we were not given extra time off to study, so every day I rose at 5.15pm, had a bath and tried to study. This didn't work. The children, on the whole, slept well, which allowed me a slice of time to look at my books; but it was hard to concentrate when I was in charge of a ward of sick infants.

*

Over the years, it had been deemed by Matron and her subordinates that as the hospital exams were considerably more difficult than those of the state, it was obligatory for the student nurses to be successful in the hospital exams before they could rise to become a Blue Belt. It was possible, but extremely rare, to be a Blue Belt at the hospital if the student had passed the hospital exams but had failed those of the state. This seemed bizarre, but rules were rules.

Before we knew it, 21st May 1962 dawned bright and sunny, and we made our way, in uniform, to the Teaching Department in Gloucester House to sit our final hospital theoretical papers in Nursing, Medicine, Surgery and Gynaecology. These papers were set by Miss Hector. We were ready. As predicted, they were difficult. The housemen and Sisters felt the exams were more suited to medical students. We weren't happy. Thank you, Miss Hector.

The vivas and practicals were much better. The vivas were a very jolly affair. I had Professor Taylor, the surgeon; Dr Black, the physician; and Mr Frazer, the gynaecologist, who I knew from my days in Outpatients. He and I had a social chat for about seven minutes and a mere three-minute gynaecology viva. Ideal. The practical examination we all agreed was passable as we had done all the procedures on the wards.

It was over; the culmination of three years' hard work had been completed.

The Final State Examinations from the General Nursing Council, for whom Miss Hector was on the Board of Examiners, were much easier and felt like a non-event. However, success in these examinations was required in order to become a State Registered Nurse (SRN).

Three weeks later in the mid-afternoon, the results of the hospital examination were posted on the noticeboard in Queen Mary's Nurses' Home. Helen the Post Keeper got very excited as she circulated the news around the hospital. We had all been hopefully, but surreptitiously, carrying our silver-buckled belts, made of navy blue grosgrain, in our baskets for several anxious days; and on hearing the news, out came the belts with the individually chosen buckle for all to admire. We became instant Blue Belts and felt very grown up. We were *Barts* Nurses!

The results of the state exams, allowing us to be called State Registered Nurses, were a foregone conclusion; and we all passed with flying colours.

A "Blue Belt" at last.

*

I now had to contemplate my future. I planned to complete my fourth year at the hospital when I would be eligible to collect my certificate and the coveted Barts badge. I knew being a Blue Belt for a year would be an invaluable experience, *but* I had just heard from David that a property had come on the market which he was in a position to buy. I felt I was ready to marry; nevertheless, there was still a large part of me that didn't want to be solely a State Registered Nurse. I also wanted my certificate, my badge and to be elected as a member of the League of St Bartholomew's Hospital Nurses.

All was not lost when suddenly Gill, another engaged member of our set, bounced into my room to tell me her news.

'We've set a date,' she announced with glee. 'I'm leaving in a month's time to get married and I can hardly wait.'

'That's so exciting,' I agreed, 'but it's a shame you're not staying for a year so you can receive your Barts badge and hospital certificate.'

'Oh, yes I will!' she replied. 'Don't you know the nuptial rules?'

'What *nuptial* rules?'

'Well, apparently, if you leave to get married – and this *only* applies to marriage – and you marry within eight weeks of leaving, this is seen as a valid reason for your departure and you are eligible to receive your hospital certificate, league membership and badge – all of which will be sent to you on your fourth anniversary.'

I couldn't believe my ears. Regrettably, I knew only a little about the League other than that it cost ten shillings to be a life member and old women in hats turned up for meetings, but being a member of the League was the criteria for earning the badge.

Within a few minutes, I had made an appointment to see

Matron, spoken to my betrothed to tell him to go ahead with the purchase of the property and had warned my parents there could be an imminent wedding.

It was only the second time I had been into Matron's office. The first was four years previously when I had been for my training interview. Nothing had changed: Miss Loveridge still sat at the same desk, still revealed her perfect, sheer black stockings encasing her swollen feet and legs, and her immaculate uniform and muslin flowing cap still remained firmly in place. I was the one who had changed. I had metamorphosed from a raw, nervous teenager into a qualified nurse, proudly wearing a navy belt with its pretty silver buckle. I was now a young woman with a fiancé. She greeted me kindly and to my astonishment was very complimentary about my work, but she was not at all surprised to hear my news. It was a very common occurrence for her nurses at this stage in their lives to choose marriage as a priority over a career. She took my resignation in her stride, and I didn't feel she was in any way concerned by my impending departure. After all, she had a host of nurses from which to choose to care for her patients.

We agreed my leaving date should be Saturday 28th July, and I explained I would be getting married on 22nd September, which was just within the tight timeframe.

The day before I left, I packed all my belongings. I couldn't resist clasping my ever-faithful childhood companion, the shabby and much-loved Bertie, to my bosom before I placed him gently in my trunk.

I reflected on just how much difference my close friends had made to my time at the hospital. We had all celebrated and commiserated in good times and bad. We planned to be godparents to our future children, and Beth gave me a beautiful silver toast rack so I could remember her necessity for her non-verbal stance at breakfast time.

There were knowing smiles all round when I was presented with a large, weightless parcel which had been wrapped with exquisite precision and tied up with a deep blue ribbon. There didn't appear to be anything in the box other than a large volume of crisp white tissue paper until a glamorous, pale blue, double layer, very décolleté negligée was revealed. 'For your trousseau,' they chorused with meaningful looks. What better friendship could there be than this?

It wasn't just my friends who had made my time at the hospital so happy and worthwhile. I was aware of the influence and example set by the nursing hierarchy at the hospital. From Matron to the "women in watchett blue", they had all played their part; and perhaps without realising it, they had shaped all our lives for the future. I knew that not only had we been taught the practical and theoretical side of nursing, but, even more significantly, despite the never-ending rules, we had been shown how important it was to put the patient first.

The next day, I received a touching final letter from my father. It was he who had originally encouraged me to keep a daily hospital journal, and I had, somewhat reluctantly, agreed. He hoped the journal hadn't dried up over the last year due to my happy personal "affair", as he knew that in the years to come, I would thank him for his yearly gift. He hoped my experience at Barts had been worthwhile and one I would look back on with pleasure and affection, and he understood it was a day tinged with some sadness for me. David: Barts, Barts: David. He appreciated that my choice was, of course, instant, natural and overwhelmingly obvious, but that it still remained bitter sweet indicated a gracious acknowledgement to Barts for allowing me to be part of it and for accepting me within its "kindly healing walls". My father was a wise man. He was right on all accounts.

27 July 1962

My dearest Greta,

I well remember writing you a letter to reach you on your first day at Barts so I thought it would be rather nice to round it all off and send you another one to reach you on your last day there. (For the record, be it said, I have also written once or twice in between!)

3¼ years! Sometimes it seems only yesterday that I saw you off at Leamington for the first (of many!) times ... sometimes it seems a deal longer.

I do so hope you have much enjoyed belonging to such a well-known

3.

and historic community. I think you have and I don't think you have any regrets whatever on the choice you made.

I hope too that it has been an experience well worth while and one you will always be able to look back on with pleasure and affection ... and I do so hope that your happy personal affair (spelt <u>without</u> an 'e' at the end, note!) of the last twelve months has not caused the 'Hospital Journal' you were keeping completely to dry up. If it has, do, somehow, in the next few weeks try to fill in the blanks. If you do this, I know, in the years to come, you will always thank me for suggesting it.

And what good friends you have made — friends Mummy and I have

3.

met and know and like to think of as our friends too. Beth, Meg, Priscilla, Anna, Mary, Jacky....

It must, in your own words, be a very bitter-sweet day for you today, my dear. David – Barts. Barts – David. Your choice is, of course, instant, natural and overwhelmingly obvious. That it still remains bitter-sweet, however, indicates not one jot of doubt but rather a gracious acknowledgment to Barts for allowing you to be part of it and for accepting you within its kindly healing walls.

.... And so, today, yet another happy era of your young life inevitably closes; but only to be the forerunner, I'm sure, of the

4.

opening of the happiest and most fulfilling period of all. And in this, as in all other things, you have Mummy's and my fondest love.

Daddy.

My father's letter written to me marking the end of my time at Barts.

A fond farewell to the patients in the Square who were enjoying the summery weather.

I finished my packing and said my "goodbyes", and David arrived to whisk me away in his economy two-door Mini, which was considered the icon of 1960s British culture. Icon it may have been, but it would barely hold all my baggage.

I took one long last look at the most "beautiful outdoor room in England" where my dreams had been realised, before I left it for what I thought was the last time.

*

The evening before my wedding, David's brother Clive arrived quite unexpectedly. With a smile on his face, he handed me an unsullied white envelope on which he had written, with perfect penmanship, *I always honour my debts.* Inside the envelope was a newly issued, crisp one pound note. I remembered immediately the prophecy he had made, as a thirteen-year-old, when we were on a double-decker bus together all those years ago, and now was I not only adding insult to injury by marrying his brother, but he was going to be David's best man!

My wedding day.

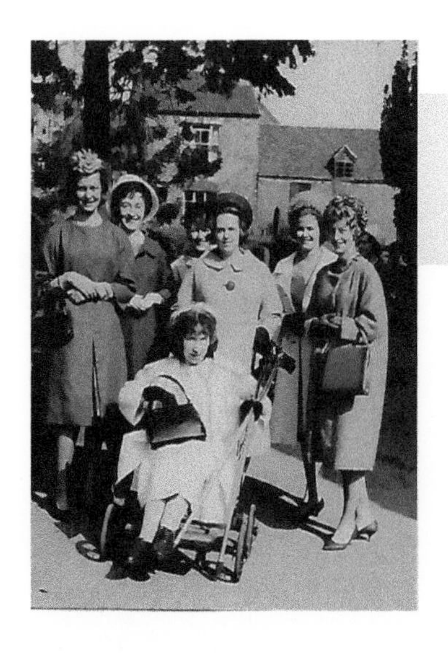

Joined by, from left:
Priscilla, Anna, Anne,
Mary, Meg and Beth
and my patient Anne.

The sun shone brightly on our wedding day in Kenilworth 22nd September 1962. I was married in the same church as many generations of my family before me. We were joined by my nursing friends and also by Anne Tucker, my special patient from Abernethy Ward. A family future beckoned.

*

On the 19th April 1963 my coveted Barts badge arrived, and I was duly elected a Life Member of the League of St Bartholomew's Hospital Nurses for the princely sum of £10. Now working locally at Stratford-upon-Avon General Hospital as a staff nurse. I pinned the badge on to my apron with pride as I realised I had achieved my goal.

A symbol of membership of The League.

Epilogue

It was one of those raw grey days when I walked from Farringdon Tube Station to the hospital. Unlike that day when I had first made this journey, I wasn't wearing a new suit or polished maroon shoes but comfortable, well-used fur boots, and I was warmly wrapped up in a camel overcoat.

As I made my way, I noticed the butchers' greasy cafés were no more, and in their place were smart white-walled modern restaurants promoting pastas, handmade focaccia, watermelon, feta salad, smoothies and goats' cheese – all very twenty-first century.

Health and Safety had obviously had a sort-out at Smithfield Meat Market, and there was less raw meat on view. To my disappointment, as I picked my way through the familiar archway, there didn't seem to be a cheerful bummaree in sight.

I stood a minute and viewed the hospital from a distance; it was good to see that the outer walls remained solid and reassuring and Henry VIII continued to look down from his elevated position exactly as he had before. This time, though, as I walked to the gate of the main entrance, there was no welcoming porter to greet me, and I went through without enquiry.

I passed the church of St Bartholomew the Less which had a notice displayed at its entrance inviting every denomination to hold their services inside; no longer was it restricted to the Church of England. The little church, sadly, was no longer a parish in its own right as the hospital didn't have any permanent residents anymore and there were no parishioners, and so it was now united with St Bartholomew the Great. I entered and saw little had changed, other than the addition of a very large book which was placed in a prominent position. Two young Muslim women were weeping as they wrote a heartfelt request. When they left, I took a look in the book and could see many poignant messages and poems from families and friends, often written in a foreign language, asking for a cure for their loved ones who were being looked after in the hospital.

I assumed the famous showpiece Square would still be majestic but no – it was a building site accommodating men wearing hard hats who were deep in conversation with each other. The elegant fountain was nowhere to be seen, and the nineteenth century plane trees had been damaged during the terrible storm of 1987 and replaced by six maples. Although the four "tryst" shelters were still in situ, they were not harbouring romantic couples; instead, they were storing building materials. Nurses and their white-coated admirers were nowhere to be seen. Everywhere felt lonely and unloved, but I could see there was work in progress, which was encouraging. The changes were perhaps unsurprising as it was 2013; and Barts, like me, was simply bearing witness to the passing of time.

I had returned not for pleasure this time, but because I had discovered a lump in my left breast. I was aware the hospital was being developed as a specialist centre in breast and cardiac care, so what better place to go to? The lump, I was sure, was benign; but it was worth a check.

I made my way to the One Stop Breast Clinic. This was housed in a renovated, very smart wing of the hospital where colourful birds, leggy storks and full moons adorned the walls.

The reception clerk, a young man, was gazing at a computer screen; and I had to remind him gently of my presence, after which he reluctantly lifted his eyes from his screen and I became a registered patient.

On my way to the changing area, I noticed a plate of mince pies on a table, above which was a notice: *MINSED [sic] PIES FOR SALE*. I smiled; it *was* Christmas after all.

In the privacy of a cubicle, I removed my outer garments and the required underwear and put on the hospital gown, briefly forgetting which way it should be worn, and whether the tapes should be done up at the front or the back. Within an instant I became an insecure patient, and the nerves began to surface. I was saved when I spotted a little old woman [who was probably my age] standing outside her cubicle, struggling for modesty's sake to do up her gown. With a sense of relief and renewed confidence, I gladly helped her and was able to escape happily, although only briefly, into the nurse's role.

I was called to the imaging department where I underwent an array of mammograms, ultrasound scans and several biopsies which were interesting, impressive and indicative of the wonders of modern technology. The very pleasant Middle Eastern consultant surgeon told me that the initial results looked "suspicious". My heart began to thud at an alarming rate. "Suspicious"? What did he mean exactly? He hadn't mentioned malignancy or cancer. Could anything else be suspicious?

I was passed on to the lovely Fatima – first names were the order of the day – who was the peripatetic Breast Care Nurse. My diagnosis was confirmed when Fatima arrived with a collection of booklets on which the word CANCER was horrifyingly obvious. In common with the surgeon, Fatima appeared to avoid using the word cancer itself, although she talked in terms of treatment choices such as lumpectomy, mastectomy, radiotherapy and chemotherapy. Evidently, the word still held its invidious power and was deemed best avoided. However, I was given an array of booklets with cancer predominant in virtually every sentence, to read in my own time.

It was a very short-lived experience being a patient at Barts during that December in 2013. Many aspects were excellent and my breast cancer was speedily diagnosed. There were, though, administrative errors regarding appointments, relevant telephone numbers and out-of-date information, and it was unnerving when I saw that one of the pathology reports had erroneously specified that the lobulated mass (lump) was located within my right breast rather than the left.

Later, on that freezing December afternoon, I left the hospital to walk back to Farringdon Tube Station: this time I was oblivious to the smart restaurants and enticing pastas, as the seriousness of my diagnosis began to dawn. I cannot remember anything about my train journey between Marylebone and Banbury other than my unsuccessful attempt to read and absorb the proffered booklets from cover to cover.

A few days later, I had to make the decision where to go for the required surgery and subsequent treatment. It was felt that the daily journey to Barts for a prolonged period was not going to work. I was disappointed; but fortunately my regret was offset when my new surgeon turned out to be a splendid and highly efficient "Barts man", which was reassuring.

*

It's June 2017, and I'm back at Barts, nearly three years after my breast cancer diagnosis, feeling fit and well. It is apparent that the splendid renovations at the hospital, both inside and out, are now nearly complete; the Square has been returned to its former glory; and cars, the scourge of today, are no longer allowed to park within its perimeter. There are ten blossoming trees, which smell sweetly as they drop their petals, and which are surrounded by colourful flowerbeds. Best of all, the fountain is once again playing prettily. New benches, strategically placed for easy conversation, have been securely screwed to the ground and overlook the water, and three circular lawns have been fashioned to surround a box hedge. It is all very beautiful apart from an abundance of cigarette butts underfoot.

I am aware that the last fifty years or so have not been easy for Barts, and the hospital has gone through a tumultuous period, especially when it was recommended that it be closed altogether. It had been argued that London's hospital services were expensive and fragmented; and many doctors and NHS managers felt that London's medical training, research and acute patient services should be on fewer sites.

In 1992, the game was up, and after over 800 years of *never* having closed its doors, Sir Bernard Tomlinson proposed the closure of the hospital. There were howls of outrage, screaming headlines in the daily newspapers, candlelit marches and prayers said in St Paul's Cathedral. The high-profile battle to save the hospital raged on, and the journalists in Fleet Street repaid the hospital for the service it had provided to them over the centuries. A petition was delivered to Downing Street signed by more than a million people, and in the end the government relented.

The Health Secretary, the full-bearded Frank Dobson, stood tall in the House of Commons and declared to his fellow MPs, 'I will not countenance the closure of that great hospital which has faithfully served the people of London for 875 years.'

Barts remained open, but the hospital had to reduce its number of beds along with many of its facilities, including the closure of the Accident and Emergency Department, and was set to specialise in cancer and cardiac care.

The hospital today is now part of Barts Health NHS Trust, the largest trust in the country, and is made up of five London hospitals which provide services, not to the East End cockney population, but to a multicultural society of two and a half million. Yes, *two and a half million*; an unwieldy number, I would imagine, to administer successfully.

Nursing also took a knock. This was due to the Salmon Report in 1966 by the Ministry of Health, which was published shortly after the retirement of our cherished Matron, Miss Loveridge. This had major implications for the structure of the nursing hierarchy as it was decided that there would be three tiers of management between the Chief Nursing Officer (no longer was she to be known as Matron) and the Sisters. No longer a *Matron*! This did not go down at all well with the Sisters at Barts as they felt their traditional autonomy was being threatened and having Nursing Officers would devalue their role. Sixty-four of them resigned between January 1968 and October 1970.

There was yet more change to come. In the latter part of the twentieth century, it was decided that to become a *registered* or "*proper*" nurse, it was compulsory to have a degree in nursing. This replaced the old system of practical ward experience interspersed with study. Rightly, or wrongly, the pioneering work of our own principal Sister Tutor, Miss Winifred Hector, had paid off and no doubt, her forward thinking had played a major role in this replacement. Today, due to the present shortage of nurses in our country, apprentice nurses have recently made a reappearance on the wards, and nurses are again "learning on the job". Following two years' full-time training, the new breed, known as nursing Associates, will plug the gap between health care assistants and qualified registered nurses to deliver hands-on care to the patients, and perhaps there will be less form-filling and computer screen viewing. I wonder if Miss Hector would have approved of this "new" system – we will never know.

In 1995, the training school at Barts was no longer made up of designated "sets" of student nurses, which had been so cherished by hundreds of young women over the years, and the Nurses' Homes were demolished. St Bartholomew's Nursing School absorbed schools from other hospitals and was incorporated into City University.

Of course, I understand that many aspects of nursing *were* different in my day, but whilst the discipline then had been harsh and some of the rules petty and unnecessary, we were never allowed to forget that compassion and care were essential even if we were unable to cure the patient. The use and value of modern technology, now in place today, cannot be disputed and has advanced medicine at a pace, but machines are inanimate and can be no substitute for tenderness and gracious manners.

It became noticeable that over the years the type of student nurse at the hospital changed. Many young women who earlier in the century would have chosen nursing as their profession, instead chose to follow other careers, including medicine, which in the past had been dominated by men. Meanwhile, new groups joined the ranks of nurses: male nurses arrived, and the ethnic mix of nurses reflected the population changes of London and the UK.

Clearly, there had to be changes at Barts to adapt to modern medical practice, and rightly so. Time moves on. The hospital is now becoming fit for purpose in the twenty-first century, and there is optimism for the future. It is evident that the much-loved hospital, which will soon have looked after patients for 900 years, never having closed its doors and never having moved, continues to thrive. Retaining its character and atmosphere, though, will be more difficult to achieve, now it is a piece of a huge organisational jigsaw.

I contemplate these issues as I sit on one of the new benches beside the fountain; the sun is shining and it's lunchtime, but all is quiet. There's scarcely a soul around, and nurses appear to be few and far between, although I'm told that many wear "scrubs" all the time these days for practicality, so they are not so easy to identify.

During my short time at Barts when I was a student nurse, I performed a very minor role indeed; in spite of this, I still felt I had *belonged* and I was *part* of a relatively small, close-knit community. I felt privileged to have completed my training at the hospital during its golden years. A warm feeling washes over me as I remember my time at the famous institution – the never-ending polishing of bedpans on night duty, the washing of all the walls on the operating theatres, the special Christmases, the devotion and sharp tongues of the Sisters, the eminent doctors and the carefree medical students and the sheer camaraderie of hospital life. Above all, I will never forget the bravery of patients like Lizzie, Anne and Matilda, who were the very reason a nursing career was so worthwhile.

I close my eyes for a minute and I can see Matron in her classic black dress and triangular cap gliding across the Square and the Sisters rushing back to their wards. I can visualise the doctors in their pristine white coats with their stethoscopes around their necks and the medical students, still loitering. I'm transported back to the day of my interview, and I can clearly see the flocks of chattering nurses in their crisp uniforms, distinguishing belts and pretty white caps as they sit on the rim of the falling fountain, perched like doves.

I open my eyes slowly and I can see the sparkling water and I can hear the tinkling fountain; and then I realise that well over half a century has passed.

The doves have flown.

Bibliography

Barnes, Greta, *Scissors, Nurse, Scissors* [Obelisk Books, Sutton-under-Brailes 2009]

Barnes, Greta and others, *The Heart of Barts* [Obelisk Books, Sutton-under-Brailes 2011]

de Savitsch, Eugene *In Search of Complications* [Andre Deutsch Ltd, London 1958]

Hector, Winifred, *Memoirs of a Somerset Woman* [Quine and Cubbon, Isle of Man 1997

Hector, Winifred and Howkins, John, *Modern Gynaecology with Obstetrics for Nurses* [William Heinemann, London 1959]

Hector, Winifred, *Modern Nursing* [William Heinemann, London 1960]

Low, Robert, *WG Grace* [Metro Publishing 2010]

Medvei, V.C. and Thornton, J.L., eds, *The Royal Hospital of Saint Bartholomew 1123- 1973* [St Bartholomew's Hospital London, London 1974]

Upton, Peter, *John O'Connell, Man of Barts* [BPAS Ltd, Hampshire]

Yeo, Geoffrey, *Nursing at Barts: A History of Nursing Service and Nurse Education at St Bartholomew's Hospital, London* [The History Press, Stroud 1995]

Acknowledgements

My thanks go to the literary agent Julian Alexander for encouraging me to expand and develop my hospital diary [*Scissors, Nurse, Scissors*] into a memoir for a wide general readership. Without his advice there would have been no book.

I am most grateful to Jo de Vries for her wise and constructive editing, Ruth Midgley and Lynne Brown for their initial encouragement and expertise, and Meg Saunders for her optimistic guidance.

The team at Matador Publishing, led by Joe Shillito, have been a pleasure to work with as has Derek Brotherton, who, along with two of my granddaughters, Millie Purton and Imogen Barnes, helped me survive the frustrations [and wonders] of computerisation.

I am indebted to Kate Jarman, the archivist at St Bartholomew's Hospital [Barts], for permission to reproduce images from the hospital archives department and to the Evening News/Associated Newspapers Ltd, as well as to Simon Brett for generously allowing the use of his beautiful wood engraving of the night nurse.

A big, big thanks to Beth Cantrell, Prilli Stevens, Sybil Allen, Mary Penny, Mary Walker, Alison Knapp, Ruth Stainton- Ellis,

Maureen Lennon, William Shand and Prof John Ashworth along with many others for their stories. I am grateful to Sir Marcus Setchell for filling me in about the future plans for Barts.

It would have been impossible to embark on *Perched Like Doves* without having shared experiences with my particularly close friends and allies: Beth Cantrell [Grunsell], Meg Toogood [Robbins], Priscilla Gurney [Russell], Mary Palmer [Gunn], Anne Hillier [Houldershaw] and the late and sorely missed Anna Barney [Nowakowska]. I continue to savour our time together. Thank you all.

I am extremely grateful to my husband David and to my son James as well as to Erica Jackson and Judith Wylie for their critical appraisal and support.